GW00645224

BORSTAL

A History of Rochester Prison

RALPH ALLISON

First Edition. Published in 2024
by Little Borstal Press
Unit 115259
PO Box 6945
London
W1A 6US

Email: littleborstalpress@gmail.com
Web: www.littleborstalpress.co.uk

Copyright © 2024 Ralph Allison

Typeset in Garamond

The moral right of the author has been asserted. All
rights reserved. No part of this publication may be
reproduced, stored in a retrieval system, or transmitted, in
any form or by any means without the prior written
permission of the publisher, nor be otherwise circulated
in any form of binding or cover other than that in which
it is published and without a similar condition being
imposed on the subsequent purchaser.

A catalogue record for this book is available from The
British Library.

ISBN: 978-1-3999-5154-8

DEDICATION

To my family, who were convinced my first book would be a complete work of fiction.

To all the staff of HM Prison Rochester – past, present, and future. You truly do change lives.

To all those who have had to hide in the shadows and are now able to be seen.

CONTENTS

ACKNOWLEDGMENTS

I acknowledge the support of Dean Gardiner MBE, current Governor of HMP Rochester.

My thanks go to the Howard League for Penal Reform and the University of Warwick for providing some early photographs of the Prison and giving permission for their inclusion in this work.

Also, the National Justice Museum (Nottingham), who provided old Borstal photographs and testimonies, the Medway Archives, Historic England, and the National Archives at Kew.

Thank you to Jill Petts for your keen eye and red pen!

I have attempted to provide references to facts where provided, but some of the history within has been passed on from conversations and may not be fully referenced.

CHAPTER 1
BORSTAL CONVICT PRISON

The first iteration of a prison at Borstal began in the 1870s. On 15 June 1871, in a question to the House of Commons, Sir Julian Goldsmid, Member of Parliament for Rochester, asked the Secretary of State for the Home Department [1]:

> *"...whether the statement is correct that it is the intention of the Government to build a Prison by means of Convict Labour on land between Gillingham and Borstal, near Rochester, which was originally purchased by the Crown for the purposes of the fortifications round London; and, if so, whether he will undertake that no further steps shall be taken in the matter without the consent of Parliament?"*

The Home Secretary, Henry Bruce MP, responded that the matter was still under consideration and that no decision would be made until Parliament had been consulted.

Borstal

The land in question was on the chalk escarpment above the tiny village of Borstal, in the largely agricultural or forested Parish of St. Margaret's (or St. Margaret's Without, that is, outside of the city walls of Rochester).

Borstal's name comes from the Anglo-Saxon *burg-steall* a 'fort site' or 'place of refuge' [2], likely referring to the steep hill which now houses Fort Borstal (see Chapter 4). However, local resident Donald Maxwell argued that a 'borstal' was a "track up a chalk hill", claiming to have heard local farmers use the term in this manner [3]. One of the earliest surviving maps of the area dates from 1769, where the village was named Bostle and was located much closer to the edge of the River Medway [4].

The village is mentioned in the Domesday Book of 1086 as Borchetelle, as land of the Bishop of Rochester [5], where six villagers were recorded, with an annual value of 10 pounds.

Public-works prisons

Edmund Du Cane was Chairman of the Board of Directors of Convict Prisons, Surveyor-general of Prisons, and Inspector-general of Military Prisons. Letters between him, the Home Office, and the War Department reveal the early planning behind the Prison's construction.

On 28th June 1872, Du Cane wrote to the Home Office requesting that a new prison be built, as the land had already been purchased by the War Department for the construction of the Chatham land defences and suggested that the convict labour could be used for such.

The plan behind the new Prison was to provide the convict labour to construct a new system of defences to protect key assets of the Medway Towns, such as the Naval Dockyard at Chatham.

"The first of a new chain of forts which will encircle Rochester and Chatham... is to be at once commenced. The work is intended to be carried out by convicts. The site selected for the fort about to be commenced is on the heights of Borstal, a suburb of Rochester, a chain of hills running in a direct line to Chatham. In order to provide the accommodation for the number of convicts who will be engaged on the fortifications, a large convict establishment for the reception of several hundred men is to be built at Rochester on land already acquired by the Government, the locality of the proposed new prison being in the parish of St. Margaret, a short distance from the city." [6]

The introduction of the public-works system in 1848 and the need to replace the prison hulks (many which had been laid up a few miles away on the Medway at Chatham and Gillingham) led to the construction of purpose-built establishments. Three public-works prisons (Portland, Portsmouth, and Chatham) were constructed between 1848 and 1856 after the abolition of transportation. The next three planned were Borstal, Chattenden and Dover. The men imprisoned in them would erect and maintain the prison buildings, manufacture items for prison use and undertake projects for the Government. Public works for the Admiralty and the War Department included creating harbours at Portland and Dover; working on the Naval dockyards at Portsmouth and Chatham; building fortifications at Portland, Borstal and Chatham; arsenals at Chatham and magazines at Chattenden [7].

In 1871, the estimated value of convict labour over expenditure for Portland, Portsmouth and Chatham was £17,759. At the same time, the Royal Engineers calculated that where work was carried out by convict labour it was much cheaper than if done by a contractor – brickwork and masonry was 40 percent cheaper, carpentry 60 percent, and earthworks 90 percent.

The original intention had been to convert the military prison, Fort Clarence, to a new convict prison, but this small site was located much closer to the city and the plan was vehemently opposed by the Corporation of Rochester and the residents. Some 1,800 prisoners were held at Chatham Convict Prison (located at what is now the Universities at Medway) and with their work on expanding the Dockyard complete, further employment was needed for them [6].

Du Cane wrote to the Home Office on 13th July 1872 highlighting that there were too many convicts being held in English prisons due to the abolition of transportation, with some 11,400 men in the system, including 2,300 in the penal colonies, who could potentially return to England for prison detention. He stated that a new public works prison was needed, to hold up to 1,000 convicts, in an area where there was space to potentially expand. The estimation was that the new prison would cost no more than £50,000 to build.

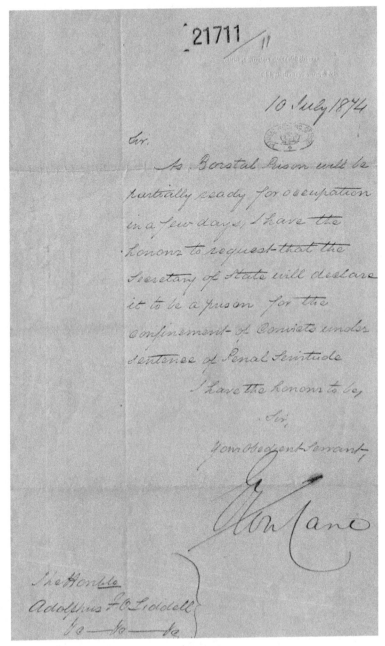

21711/11

10 July 1874

Sir.

As Borstal Prison will be partially ready for occupation in a few days, I have the honour to request that the Secretary of State will declare it to be a prison for the confinement of Convicts under sentence of Penal Servitude

I have the honour to be,

Sir,

Your Obedient Servant

Du Cane

The Honble
Adolphus F. O. Liddell
&c — &c — &c

The letter from Du Cane announcing the Prison is nearly ready to occupy [8].

4

Construction and early days

The land was compulsory purchased by the War Department for the Crown from the Rochester Bridge-wardens, by way of the Defence Act of 1860. According to the minutes of the Rochester Bridge-wardens in 1862, the land was purchased *"for the purpose of National Defences"*. They requested compensation of £5,939 (approximately £574,700 in today's money) from the Government as the land included part of a farm being occupied by one of their tenant farmers, and land used for a wood supply [9].

On 10th April 1873, Du Cane wrote that as the proposed site was not surrounded by water or stone, as was the case for the other public works prisons, suitable fencing would be needed to secure the perimeter, as well as the cutting down of adjacent woodland. The next month, the War Department replied agreeing that the land between Borstal and Cookham Wood may be used, temporarily, for the construction of the Prison, and gave permission for the woodland to be felled, but they advised that Du Cane contact the Royal Engineers for the construction of the fencing and provision of tools.

Three months later in July, Du Cane wrote to the Home Office stating that Borstal Prison would be partially ready for occupation in a few days and asked that the Secretary of State declare it officially a prison.

On 16th July 1874, by Her Majesty's Command, a royal warrant was signed officially designating Borstal as a place of confinement for male offenders under sentence or order of transportation, and for male offenders sentenced or ordered to be kept in penal servitude.

The Prison officially opened on 3rd August 1874 when a small working party of male convicts arrived from Chatham Convict Prison [10] and stayed their first night. For 16 weeks prior to this first night, they had been transported the 4-mile distance from Chatham daily in secure wagons until such a time that secure accommodation was built for the 40 [11], a wooden perimeter fence having already been constructed by free labour. The convicts selected to transfer were chosen on account of their "good character and their knowledge of useful trades, all of the first-class, and their time nearly expired" [12]. On 14th October, the total number of convicts was made up to 100 on completion of A Hall [13].

"Borstal Prison is new on the list. It was opened in August 1874 by the conveyance thither of 40 convicts from Chatham, selected on account of their good conduct; supplies for the prisoners were daily forwarded from Chatham Prison. The situation of Borstal Prison is high and healthy, and the prisoners greatly improved in condition there. Much convict labour was employed in erecting the buildings." [14]

In February 1875, Borstal was included in a central request to tender for supplies of food, provisions, and stores by Directorate of Convict Prisons.

CONTRACTS FOR SUPPLIES FOR CONVICT PRISONS.

PERSONS desirous of TENDERING for the SUPPLY of MEAT, Wheat, Flour, Barley, Oatmeal, Wines, Spirits, Ale, &c., Coals, Coke, and Firewood, Groceries, Provisions, Cheese. Tea, Milk, Fowls, and Eggs, Vegetables, Soap, Candles, and oilman's Stores, Bedding Clothing and Materials, Cutlery, Ironmongery and Tinware, Leather, and Grindery, Brushes, Brooms, Mops, Crockeryware and Glass, Weaving Tools, Wefts and Warps, Drugs, and Sundries, &c., for twelve months, from the 1st April next, for the use of Convicts confined in Her Majesty's Convict Prisons at Borstal, Brixton, Chatham, Dartmoor, Fulham, Millbank, Parkhurst, Pentonville, Portland, Portsmouth, Wormwood-scrubs, and Woking (male and female in one tender), may obtain forms of Tender on and after MONDAY, 1st FEBRUARY, by applying at the several Prisons, or at the Office of Directors of Convict Prisons, No. 44, Parliament-street, Westminster, S.W.

Samples may be seen and inspected on application at this Office, Millbank, Pentonville, and the other Prisons. Separate Tenders for each Prison (on printed forms only), duly signed by the parties tendering and two referees, to be addressed and forwarded (prepaid) to the Directors of Convict Prisons, No. 44, Parliament-street, Westminster, S.W., marked "Tenders for Convict Prison Supplies," on or before Twelve o'clock Noon, on SATURDAY, FEBRUARY 20th, 1875.

The Parties whose Tenders are accepted will be notified thereof. No Tender will be considered unless made on the new schedules for 1875-6.

Dated 44, Parliament-street, 15th January, 1875.

[371]

A newspaper tender request in the Dorset County Chronicle, 4 February 1875.

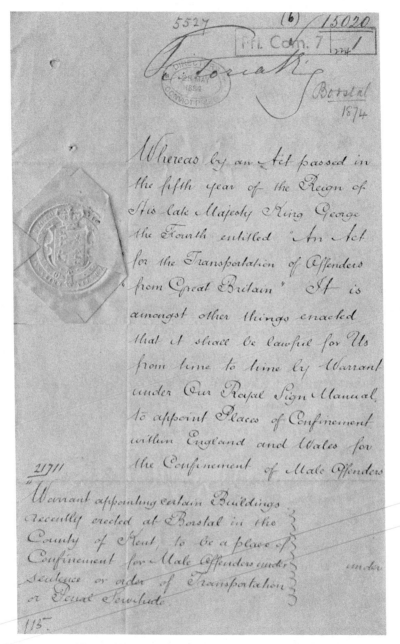

The Royal Warrant officially authorising Borstal Convict Prison [15].

In April 1875, several convicts were transferred to Borstal from Pentonville to increase the labour force. Over 100 were chiefly employed on the construction works, and those not required on the works were engaged in cultivating the land surrounding the Prison (some 10 acres) with potatoes and cabbages.

An additional £5,000 was requested from the Treasury and proposed to Parliament to continue the construction, and it was calculated that the Prison would cost £3,806 to run in the year 1875-76. As part of this proposal, they broke down the annual salaries of the new staff as below – current values provided using Bank of England inflation calculations [16].

Position	1875 Salary	2023 value
Governor	£400	£38,132
Deputy-governor	£300	£28,600
Chaplain	£200	£19,066
Medical officer	£300	£28,600
First-class clerk	£140 (+£25)	£15,730
Second-class clerk	£80	£7,630
Second-class schoolmaster	£80	£7,630
Chief warder	£100	£9,530
Principal warder (x2)	£68	£6,480
Warder (x8)	£58	£5,530
Assistant warder (x12)	£55	£5,240
Instructing officer	£68	£6,480
Infirmary warder	£68	£6,480
Infirmary asst. warder (x2)	£50	£4,770
Cook	£50	£4,770
Night watchman (x2)	£50	£4,770
Gatekeeper	£68	£6,480
Asst. Gatekeeper	£58	£5,530
Foreman of works	£73	£6,960
Labourer/messenger	£50	£4,770

With the labour available, it was expected that all construction work at the Prison be completed by the end of 1875.

Chatham Convict Prison produced a great many of the fittings which were then conveyed to the Borstal site via barge which docked at a pier on the River Medway and then via a narrow-gauge railway up the hill (see Chapter 4). By May 1875, the Prison Commission determined that Chatham Prison could not supply enough materials to keep up with construction at Borstal, so put out a request to tender for bricks, gravel, and sand.

BRICKS, GRAVEL, AND SAND.
PERSONS desirous of Tendering for the SUPPLY of the above materials to the 31st day of March, 1876, to be delivered at the New Convict Prison at Borstal, near Rochester, are requested to forward their Tenders, prepaid, addressed to the Surveyor-General of Prisons, 44, Parliament-street, on or before WEDNESDAY, the 26th day of MAY, 1875.

Forms of tender will be supplied on application at Borstal Prison, or at the office of the Surveyor-General of Prisons, 44, Parliament-street, S.W.

44, Parliament-street, 12th May, 1875.

A request for tender published in the South Eastern Gazette on 17 May 1875.

By the end of 1876, it was reported that Borstal had cells for 500 prisoners, with stores, offices, a temporary infirmary, and quarters for eighteen warders already constructed [11].

Building work continued into the 1880s. The four cell blocks were all occupied by 1877, and the punishment cells (later known as the Segregation Unit) was completed in 1878 – this is the oldest original building remaining on the site today.

The kitchen, bakehouse and bathhouse were completed in 1880. The permanent infirmary was finished between 1883-4 and the Chapel was first used in July 1884. A temporary workshop for tailors and shoemakers was erected in 1880 and then enlarged the following year [7].

Borstal differed from the previous convict prisons in both layout and construction. The prison had a radial plan, with four detached cell blocks radiating out from a central area containing the kitchen and chapel. The wings were single-storey, with 14-inch-thick brick outer walls, corrugated-iron roofs, timber corridor walls and corrugated-iron cell partitions. Each wing contained 126 sleeping cells, each measuring 9ft x 4ft 9in x 7ft 6in high (2.7 x 1.4 x 2.3m) making a total of 504 cells.

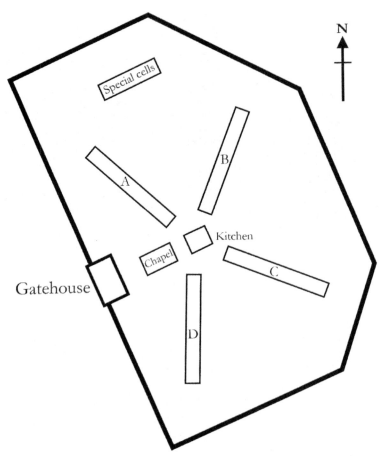

A plan of the original layout of Borstal Convict Prison, prior to construction of ancillary buildings.

Each wing had a ten-foot-wide central corridor with 63 cells on each outer wall. They were heated with three large Gurney stoves in the corridor, and each cell door had a louvred panel at the bottom which allowed the heated air to pass into the cell. Each stove was supplied with fresh air from outside the building using large channels, and each cell had a shaft which ventilated air out via the roof – the draw of this air was assisted by a gas lamp inside the cell. Halfway up the hall on each side there was a recess in which were two toilets for use by prisoners when on the wing [17].

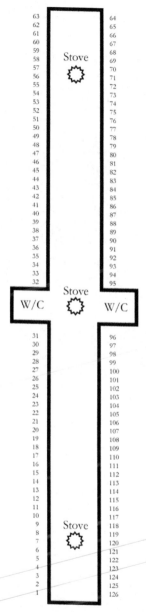

A plan of each wing with cell numbers, based on a lithograph by Thomas Tannahill in 1890.

*Exterior shot of buildings at Borstal. 1902. In the foreground is A Hall. In the midground
you can see the Chapel and its clock tower (which still stand today).
Howard League / University of Warwick (MSS.16A/7/23/1/27a-c)*

*Left. Inside the landing of a
cellblock. 1902.*

*The landings step up to account
for the lay of the land – being at
the top of a hill, it's not a flat
site.*

*The stoves would have been the
only source of heat, aside from the
meagre gas lights which hang
from the ceiling.*

*Howard League / University of
Warwick
(MSS.16A/7/23/1/1a-b)*

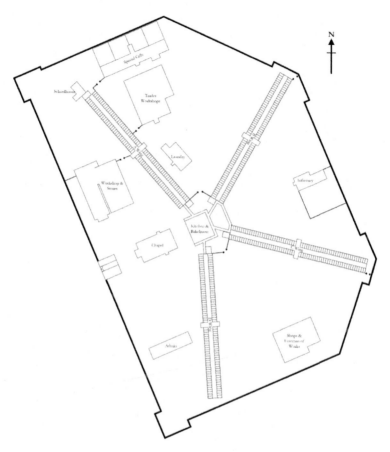

Layout of the Prison prior to reconstruction work started by the juvenile-adults in 1908.

Cell windows measured 1'6" x 1'6" (about 46 x 46cm), with a flap on the inside to allow in fresh air and no guard bars, which gave convicts a dreary outlook. According to the custom for prisons at the time, their size only allowed in half the amount of daylight that they should have.

There was no call bell system available to convicts – to attract the attention of a warder, they needed to thrust their cap out below the door. Obviously, this only worked if a warder was watching out!

Before the building of the bathhouse, at the inner end of each cell block there were 6 baths sunk into the ground, lined with concrete, a style used in early convict prisons.

The special cells block was a heavy, sombre, two-storeyed brick building. In it was a justice room (for delivering sentence on misdemeanours), 6 ordinary cells, 3 lobbied cells and one padded cell fitted with waterproof sheeting. On the top floor were twelve more ordinary cells. Behind the block were four small, closed yards where convicts were permitted to exercise in solitary.

Life in the convict prison

As a public-works prison, life for convicts mostly revolved around the construction of the prison itself in the early years, and later the construction of the defensive forts in the local area. But that was not the case for all the convicts at Borstal. Many convicts had been assigned to turn over the area of land surrounding the prison to agriculture from early 1875. This was so successful, that by December, the Governor was offering a bumper crop of cabbages for sale to successful bidders (though not necessarily the highest).

CABBAGES FOR SALE.

TENDERS at so much per cwt. are invited for the purchase of nearly the whole of the CABBAGES now growing on the land of the Borstal Convict Prison.

The cabbages will be cut and weighed by prison labor, but they must be carted away at the expense of the purchaser, and in reasonably convenient quantities.

Tenders, addressed to the Governor, H.M. Convict Prison, Borstal, will be received up to 12 noon on the 9th December; and the cabbages may be viewed any week day between the hours of 10 and 3, on application to the Steward.

Neither the highest nor any tender will necessarily be accepted.

The Governor advertised the sale of the bumper crop of cabbages in the South Eastern Gazette on 6 December 1875.

Farming was to become a massive engagement of labour at the Prison, and a useful source of income too. In 1875, eleven acres of ground were cultivated with potatoes, carrots, turnips, onions, and cabbages, with a favourable yield (as above) apart from the onions. In 1876, some fifty acres were cropped, but with a less favourable

14

harvest, which the Governor put down to lack of rainfall and poor land caused by the previous tenants [18]. Later in 1896-97, 27.5 acres were planted with barley, wheat, grass (for hay) and root vegetables, but the stock of pigs were struck down with swine fever and had to be disposed of. The plan was to reconstruct the pigsties elsewhere, but by 1898 the decision had been made to discontinue pig-keeping entirely and demolish the old sties.

The prison regime

To maintain discipline amongst the prison population (including the staff), a strict regime was adhered to. There were a series of electrically operated bells in the halls, workshops, and externally, which were used to signal the next change in the routine (although, due to noise, the bells were not used at certain times of the day).

Weekdays were an early start at 5 o'clock for breakfast and then prayers (first on the halls, but when the Chapel was constructed both staff and prisoners would pray together here daily), followed by two sessions of labour, punctuated with lunch. After second labour, prisoners would undertake schooling and letter writing for 45 minutes, as well as the issuing of kit and the searching of both prisoners and cells. After the prisoners were locked in their cells, the officers would leave (leaving the night patrols and reserve guard) and the prison would be locked up at 8pm.

Saturdays generally followed the same weekday morning structure without labour, and after lunch there was the opportunity to bathe, for haircuts, for kit exchange and more searching of cells and prisoners. This was cleaning day, and cells and halls were thoroughly cleaned, and stores organised neat and tidy.

On Sundays, prisoners were permitted a two-hour lie-in, rising at 7 o'clock. After breakfast there were morning and afternoon sessions of Chapel, general parade, and exercise. Here, prisoners received spiritual enlightenment, as well as access to fresh air as part of their physical exercise.

Warders and officers worked in three shifts, consisting of short duty (from around 7am until 6pm, roughly today's Main shift), full duty (from 5am to around 7pm, today's A shift) and the night patrol, with the duties of each also being managed by the regime.

Feb 16 – 31 Oct	Nov 1 – 15 & Feb 1 – 15	Nov 16 – Jan 31	Duties performed
05:00	05:15	05:30	Bell rings; prisoners rise; wash; dress; make beds and sweep cells.
05:20	05:35	05:50	Officers (division on full duty) parade for muster in halls; roll called; keys issued; slops collected; muster of prisoners taken; names taken for medical officer; cells, wards and halls swept; and a certain number of cells and prisoners searched.
05:40	05:55	06:10	Breakfast brought over from cook and bakehouses and issued.
06:00	06:15	06:30	Officers on full duty leave for breakfast; breakfast patrols take charge.
06:40	06:55	07:15	Officers on full duty return from breakfast; muster in halls; slops collected; and prisoners unlocked for chapel.
06:45	07:00	07:20	Bell commences ringing for prayers; prisoners file in.
06:50	07:05	07:25	Prisoners having assembled in chapel and halls, prayers commenced.
07:00	07:15	07:35	Officers (division on short duty) enter prison and parade for inspection; prisoners parade for labour, and march out when ready.
	11:10		Bell rings for recall from labour.
	11:30		Prisoners' dinner served out; second relief of dinner patrols leave for dinner.
	11:45		Officers leave for dinner; first relief of dinner patrols take charge.
	12:15		Second relief dinner patrols return and take charge; first relief leave for dinner.
	12:45		Officers return from dinner and parade for inspection.
	12:55		Prisoners parade for labour and march out when ready.
	13:00		First relief dinner patrols return and join the labour parade.

Feb 16 – Oct 15	Oct 16 – 31 & Feb 1 – 15	Nov 1 – Dec 31	Jan 1 – Jan 31	Duties performed
17:15	16:45	16:00	16:15	Bell rings for recall from labour.
17:35	17:05	16:20	16:35	Officers (division on full duty) leave for supper; prisoners suppers served out; names taken for Governor, Chaplain, and

18:05	17:35	16:50	17:05	for repairs of clothing.
				Officers (division on full duty) return to the prison; division on short duty leave for the night; prisoners unlocked for schooling and letter writing; slops collected; water served out; clothing issued; cells and prisoners searched; general ward duties attended to.

18:50	All prisoners are locked up in their cells; locking up reports made out and keys collected; night patrols and reserve guard parade and are posted; one of the latter posted in each hall until 8pm, when they assemble in the guard room for the night.
19:00	All officers (except night patrols and reserve guard) leave the prison.
19:45	Prisoners make down hammocks and turn in.
19:55	Lights out.
20:00	Lock up prison.

On Saturdays (throughout the Year)

Duties up to 11:45 as on other weekdays. Officers (short duty) do not return after leaving for dinner.

12:45	Officers (division on full duty only) return and parade for inspection; prisoners bathed; hair cut; cells and prisoners searched; halls generally cleaned; clean kits issued; ward duties performed.
17:35	Prisoners' supper served out.
17:50	Officers go to supper, except supper patrol as detailed on roster.
18:30	Officers on duty return and lock up prisoners; locking up reports made out and keys collected.
18:50	Night patrol and reserve guard posted as on other days; and remaining duties at same hours as on other weekdays.

Sundays (throughout the Year)

07:00	Bell rings; prisoners rise; wash and sweep cells.
07:05	Officers (division on duty) parade for muster in the halls; roll called; slops collected.
07:40	Prisoners' breakfasts issued.
07:55	Officers leave for breakfast; breakfast patrols take charge.
08:55	Officers' parade.
09:00	Officers march to halls; keys issued; slops collected.
09:10	Chapel; general parade and exercise. Until 12:30.
12:35	Prisoners' dinner served out.
12:45	Officers leave for dinner; dinner patrols take charge.
13:45	Officers return from dinner; keys issued; dinner tins collected.
13:55	Chapel; general parade and exercise. Until 16:45.
16:50	Prisoners' suppers served out.
17:00	Officers leave for supper; supper patrols take charge.
18:30	Officers return; keys issued; ward duties.
18:45	Prisoners make down hammocks and turn in.
18:55	Lights out.
19:00	Lock up prison; officers leave.

The daily regime at Borstal in 1876.

Prison labour

Many trades were available to the convicts at Borstal, part of a system designed to reduce reoffending by ensuring that men left prison with a skilled trade, meaning they were more likely to gain meaningful employment upon release.

Convict labour was generally split between War Department work (the Eastern Defences), work on the prison buildings, working on the farms and general prison labour (such as cooking, cleaning, and tailoring).

A convict at Borstal could be trained in any of the following trades, affording him a route out of crime upon his release:

- Excavation works, including heavy excavation and concreting
- Bricklaying
- General or light labourer
- Carpentry and joinery
- Sawyer
- Blacksmithing and fitting
- Stonemason
- Slater
- Plasterer
- Painter
- Glazier
- Farmer
- Bookbinder
- Tailor
- Tinman
- Washer
- Shoemaker
- Cook
- Baker
- Cleaner

We can gain a fascinating amount of information about how convict labour was used at Borstal from the Annual Report from the Governor to the Directors of Convicts Prison.

Employment of Convicts.

Nearly one half of the prisoners have been since August employed on the Royal Engineer works. Of the rest, about one half are employed on prison works, new buildings etc; and the remainder, deducting a few employed in the necessary duties of the prison, in cultivating the land.

Public Works.

For the Royal Engineer Department a road has been made nearly a mile in length, of an average width of 20 feet, from the site of the fort to the river.

Excavations and tunnelling have been made for water pipes from the main in Borstal to the fort.

A tank has been excavated 30 feet deep and 25 feet square, and a meter house erected. Of the work done on the fort, the gorge ditch has been dug of the length of 778 feet, 25½ feet wide, and average depth of 8½. The ditch of right face has been dug to a length of 486 feet, 25½ wide, and 20 feet deep.

The front face 196 feet in length, 25½ in width and 10½ feet deep.

The excavated chalk has been wheeled up to form parapets, and the loam collected into spoil heaps ready for covering them when completed. The flint has also been collected, and some broken and used for concreting.

Offices, store, smith shops, stable, and coach-house have been erected, as well as a shelter-shed for convicts, and stages for the civil guard.

Prison Works.

The quarters for the subordinate officers (2 principal warders and 18 warders) are many of them, so far as the building is concerned, ready for occupation, and are now only awaiting the adoption of a system of drainage.

One house for a superior officer is also well advanced as far as the brickwork is concerned, and orders have recently been received for the commencement of another similar one.

The offices for the steward and steward's clerk were completed and occupied during the month of December, and the adjoining stores are progressing. The water has been laid on to a well within the boundary fence, from which it is pumped into a tank near the centre, from which the prison is supplied.

A portion of the ground within the fence has been enclosed for an artisans' yard, and the fence round it is nearly completed.

Of the halls, A and D remain as last year, except that the interiors have been varnished, and the cell doors of the former painted. A portion of B hall was occupied in August by 68 additional prisoners, and during the month of December the sick were permanently removed to an infirmary at one end of that hall. The remaining cells, 30 in number, are now ready for occupation. C hall alone remains in an unfinished state. The greater portion of it is at present taken up by the steward's stores and the root crops, for which, at present, there is no other place. This hall could be completed in some three months' time, should it be necessary.

Farm.

Upwards of 50 acres of land were cultivated during the past year. The crops were hardly satisfactory, but were, I believe, nearly equal to those of our immediate neighbours.

The weather of the early part of the year was much against all the crops, which suffered from want of rain for some months after the sowing. The result has been a balance of some £200 over the expenditure – a sum I trust, with favourable weather and additional experience, to far exceed next season. The land, however, is very poor, and some portion of it was, before being acquired by us, let to farmers as yearly tenants, who, knowing the probably short duration of their tenancy, obtained as much as they could out of the land without going to any expense in respect of it.

Pigsties were erected during the latter part of the year, and five sows were obtained from Woking Prison. Three have recently littered, and our numbers are now 25.

Extract from the Report to the Directors of Convict Prisons, 1877 (for the year 1876).

Meaningful employment within the Prison gave the convicts not only the hope of a better life, but also earnings to spend inside. The next few tables show examples of the average earnings for some of the work completed at Borstal, also in 1876.

PRISON BUILDINGS.

Employment	No. days	Av. Earnings per man per day		Annual total		
		s.	d.	£	s.	d.
Labourers	3,305	2	0	330	10	0
Light labour	395	0	6	9	17	6
Bricklayers	664	2	6	82	19	4
Carpenters	568	2	5¾	70	6	6
Smith and fitter	656	2	5¾	81	8	9
Painters	1,429	2	8½	163	8	6
Total	7,017	2	1¼	738	10	7

THE FARM.

Employment	No. days	Av. Earnings per man per day		Annual total		
		s.	d.	£	s.	d.
Cropping, etc.	5,901	1	0	295	1	0
Sundry repairs	26	2	6¼	3	5	9
Total	5,927	1	0	298	6	9

SERVICE OF THE PRISON.

Employment	No. days	Av. Earnings per man per day		Annual total		
		s.	d.	£	s.	d.
Labourers	118	1	10¼	11	0	8
Light labour	314	0	6	7	17	0
Carpenter	64	2	5¼	7	16	8
Fitter	25	2	3¼	2	16	11
Tailors	1,846	4	5¼	410	13	6
Shoemakers	883	1	8	73	16	11
Bookbinders	466	2	6	58	5	0
Washers	2,101	1	3¾	138	14	4
Tinmen	108	1	5¼	7	16	10
Bakers	1,243	2	6	155	7	6
Cooks	1,556	2	6	194	10	0
Stoker	311	2	0	38	17	6
Cleaners	3,345	2	0	334	10	0
Total	12,380	2	4	1442	3	0

By way of an inflation-based comparison to today:

1876	£1 (pound)	s. 1 (shilling)	d. 1 (pence)
2023	£95.33	£4.68	£0.39

Education

The Directors of Convict Prisons deemed education an integral part of the rehabilitation of convicts, especially at Borstal. In the early years of the Prison, education was overseen by the Prison Chaplain and delivered by a single schoolmaster, at least in the early years.

In 1876, the Chaplain reported that he was not able to make much progress in educating convicts because the one schoolmaster he had was not sufficient, and that he was hindered by school equipment (or the lack of).

"A good library is also a great desideratum; and as I feel sure that it would be much appreciated, both by officers and men, I venture to hope that the present old and well-worn selection will ere long be supplanted by a fuller and more suitable supply." Taken from the Report to the Directors of Convict Prisons, 1876 (for the year 1875).

Convicts were taught the three Rs – reading, writing and arithmetic (or reading, 'riting and 'rithmetic!) and were graded on a standard scale of 0-6. At the end of 1875, the Chaplain reported the status of 196 prisoners as below.

EDUCATIONAL STATUS OF 196 PRISONERS AT BORSTAL, 31 DECEMBER 1875.

STANDARD	READING	WRITING	ARITHMETIC
0	4	3	4
1	3	3	19
2	11	38	37
3	17	79	47
4	70	47	55
5	62	14	19
6	29	12	15

To summarise the educational abilities of the convicts, a simpler system was also used.

	READING	WRITING	ARITHMETIC
Very ignorant	7	6	23
Partially educated	28	117	84
Fairly educated	70	47	55
Well educated	91	26	34

It is clear from these figures that convicts were not entirely the uneducated layabouts that have been alluded to in the past, at least not at Borstal. The trades on offer, such as bricklaying and carpentry were and still are heavily reliant on the use of mathematics for materials' measurement, calculating angles and quantity surveying.

A year later, the books that the Chaplain demanded had arrived, and were reportedly read with *"much avidity"*. He noted that he was pleased with the progress in education, more so in arithmetic, but that progress was less favourable in reading and spelling from dictation. Again, he stresses that the situation will not improve without additional staff to support him in delivering education.

By 1897, the Chaplain was in a much better position for education delivery. Every prisoner was issued with a bible, a prayer book, and a hymn book. If desired, he could have a special devotion book, which was changed monthly. He was also permitted two library books (changed once a week) and four educational books (changed every two months). Those prisoners that showed exceptional intelligence were allowed to have their educational books changed more frequently (subject to permission of the Director).

The additional books and staffing clearly made a difference. The table below shows the educational status of 153 prisoners at Borstal up until 31st March 1897, with standards on conviction compared to that on discharge.

STANDARD	READING		WRITING		ARITHMETIC	
	CONV.	DIS.	CONV.	DIS.	CONV.	DIS.
0	3	0	5	0	7	1
1	2	3	3	1	30	23
2	8	2	9	4	42	39
3	12	8	35	32	23	16
4	48	40	50	43	27	39
5	50	51	31	42	7	9
6	30	49	20	31	17	26

I have not yet approached the subject of religious practice but combined with education it appears to have had a marked impact on the lives of some prisoners. In 1898, the Chaplain received the following letter from a rector, relating to a recently discharged prisoner:

"Dear Sir, I have to thank you in the name of R.K., and also on my own account, for your kindness and good advice to him, both during his imprisonment at Borstal and also on his leaving for home on Wednesday the 15th instant. K. desires me to send you his best thanks for advice, kindness, and the books. He showed me the letter with some pride, and I only hope he will continue as he has begun. He appears altogether an improved and altered man, and I trust that his punishment may have a real and lasting good effect. He seems grateful generally for the kindness shown him while in prison." Taken from the Report to the Directors of Convict Prisons, 1898-99.

Prisoner uniforms

Prison uniform consisted of a white jacket, trousers, and pillbox hat, all stamped with the broad arrow to denote Crown property. The idea of covering the uniforms of penal servitude prisoners with the broad arrow was first introduced by Sir Edmund Du Cane in the 1870s after his appointment as Chairman of Convict Directors and Surveyor-General of Prisons. Du Cane considered the broad arrow to be a hindrance to escape and a mark of shame.

As a public-works prison, convicts at Borstal were also issued with boots. One prisoner described the boots:

"Fully fourteen pounds in weight. I put them on and the weight of them served to fasten me to the ground. It was not that alone, but the sight of the impression they left on the gutter as you looked at the footprints of those who walked before you, struck terror to your heart. There was the felon's brand of the 'broad arrow' impressed on the soil by every footstep... the nails in the soles of your boots and shoes were hammered in an arrow shape, so that whatever ground you trod you left traces that Government property had travelled over it." [19].

Wormwood Scrubs prison, London: four cooks in prison uniform standing in a line in front of buckets and baskets. Process print after P. Renouard, 1889. Wellcome Collection.

A 19ᵗʰ Century prisoner uniform, on display at the museum at Fort Luton.

Warder uniforms

Prison warder uniform was made of the same dark blue or black melton (woollen) cloth as police uniforms and had a similar cut. The hats were described as either kepis or shakos and were of a similar French design to those worn by American forces in the American Civil War. Badges and insignia varied between prisons, but Borstal uniform from 1902 featured the crown badge on the front of the cap. Buttons and belt buckles had a small crown in the centre surrounded by 'HM Prison' in either brass or white metal. Boots were a military style with metal studs in the soles.

Many officers were issued with police-style whistles on chains to raise the alarm if necessary. Their keys were attached to their belt by a spring clip chain, the keys themselves kept in a leather pouch on the belt, a tradition which, along with the Acme City whistle, continues today.

Principal warders were denoted by a crown backed by a starburst on the collar and the chief warder wore a wire badge of a crown surrounded by laurels. All warders were expected to be 'clean and presentable' [20].

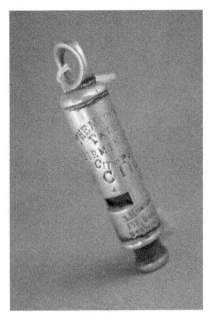

The early style of prison-issued whistle [21].

The birch and the cat

Corporal punishment was commonplace at convict prisons, and Borstal was no exception to this. The birch was used on convicts who seriously broke prison rules, such as assaulting a warder. The Governor was not permitted to order that a prisoner be flogged, instead it had to be brought before the Visiting Justices who could impose an order of flogging [20].

Portrait of a warder at Borstal. 1902.
Howard League / University of Warwick (MSS.16A/7/23/1/30a-b)

The 'birch' was a bundle of leafless twigs from the birch tree, harvested in winter when the sap is down. There was no specification for the number of twigs to use, but surviving examples suggest it was probably between fifty and seventy young twigs about 3ft in length. The cut ends were bound with cotton or sisal twine to make a handle, with the flogging being delivered by the thinner ends.

Traditionally, the birch was soaked in brine before use, which increased the weight, flexibility, and strength of the twigs, making the punishment issued much more severe in terms of pain and damage to the flesh. The brine had antibacterial qualities, which helped to prevent infection developing in the resulting wounds.

In some prisons, a wooden apparatus known as a birching donkey or birching pony was constructed specially for birching. The prisoner would lay over the donkey with legs held together, taking care not to strike the back of the genitals.

A birching stool from around 1899. National Justice Museum, Nottingham [22].

The cat o' nine tails, oft shortened to 'cat', is a multi-tailed whip which first saw use in the Royal Navy. The first cats were made up of nine knotted thongs of cotton cord, about 75cm (2½ ft) in length, designed to lacerate the skin and inflict pain. The number nine comes from the rope that was initially used, which was cable laid. This had 9 strands in total, a result of the laying of three hawser laid ropes (which had three strands in each).

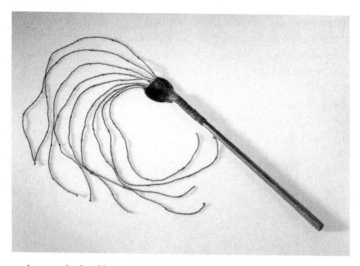

An example of a 19ᵗʰ century cat o' nine tails as used by the Royal Navy (Science Museum, London).

Birching and the use of the cat, as a judicial punishment, was outlawed in 1948. But it was still used as a punishment for violent breaches of prison discipline, such as mutiny or attacking staff, until 1962, although not officially outlawed until 1967.

A 1951 memorandum ordered all UK male prisons to use only cat o' nine tails and birches from a national stock at Wandsworth prison, where they were to be thoroughly tested before being supplied to a prison where flogging was pending for use in discipline [23]. These regulation cats had a total weight of 9oz, with each 'tail' made of 33 inches of fine whipcord, bound with silk at the tip, attached to a 19in handle.

A "well conducted", recently released prisoner wrote to the Sheffield Independent in 1879, to explain in his experience of how the cat was administered in convict prisons.

"At about nine or ten o'clock in the morning of the day after the sentence has been read, the culprit is marched, guarded by several warders, to a large room near the "chain room"... he is there stripped of all clothing except the knickerbocker breeches, gagged and fastened at the wrists by iron rings, and at the ankles by stout leather straps, to the iron triangles... The warder selected to administer the lashes then prepares himself for the task, for which he will receive 2s. 6d. extra pay and a half day on leave of absence. The "cat" is handed to the

operating warder... and all being pronounced "ready", the order is given to "lay on", the chief warder loudly counting the strokes. The decreed number of lashes having been duly inflicted, the culprit is unbuckled and laid face downwards, upon a mattress if very weak; if not, a jacket is thrown over his shoulders and he is marched back to the punishment cell, or taken to the infirmary, where his back is plastered with healing ointment and a large sheet of thin sheet lead is fastened to the bare back by a piece of stout cord passing round the front of the throat and through two holes in the sheet of lead, each hole being opposite each shoulder." [24]

An example of a "triangle" on which a convict to be corporally punished was secured, said to look like a painter's ladder. Image by 'Merryjack' on Flickr (CC BY-SA 2.0)

Sometimes neither the birch nor the cat was enough of a deterrent for serious misdemeanours by convicts at Borstal. In 1904, convict George Williams, whilst being part of a working party marching toward Fort Borstal, attacked a warder with a spade, with one blow cutting out a piece of his kneecap and leaving him unable to walk. A court heard that Williams' excuse was that Warder Blandford was kicking prisoners' dinners into their cells, which Blandford denied. Williams was lucky that other prisoners had held back the attending Principal Warder, who would have cut him down otherwise [25].

The cost of managing crime

In an order for a second reading of a proposed Prisons Bill in the House of Commons on 22 June 1876, Peter Rylands, MP for Burnley stated that the population of Borstal was 315 men with a cost per head of £55 per year. The average salary at Borstal was £120 per year. This was to illustrate the disparity in costs between local gaols and those under Government control, where the average cost per prisoner was £50 in state prisons, but only £27 in locals [26]. Later, all prisons would come under state control, but today arguments are still being had about the differences in costs to manage prisoners in state and privately run prisons.

An epidemic spread

In early 1890, Borstal was the site of a major outbreak of influenza, as Thomas Tannahill, Medical Officer at Borstal wrote in the Glasgow Medical Journal.

From 7th January, the number of convicts displaying symptoms steadily grew until it peaked on 29th January with 29 cases, where it gradually declined until the middle of February. Tannahill studied all the cases presenting to him, which included members of staff, and proposed that the disease entered the prison from Borstal village. Specifically, a young girl who came down with the illness on 25th December 1889, who happened to be the daughter of a warder, who himself became infected but on finding it affected him slightly, he dismissed it and continued his duties at the prison. Mixing freely with the prisoners, this then led to the outbreak [17].

Little was known about the cause of influenza at the time, and viruses were not isolated until 1892 at the earliest, so Tannahill's paper and its in-depth research methods show incredibly good practice at infection mapping and epidemiology.

The lithographs drawn in his journal article represent the best visual evidence of the layout of the earliest wings at Borstal.

Preparing for a new enemy

By the beginning of the 20th century, the political landscape in

Europe had changed. No longer was France the enemy that had warranted the construction of the Eastern Defences (Chapter 4), as relations were warming toward the signing of the *Entente cordiale* in 1904. Instead, a new threat was looming, that from a new Imperial Germany, who, decades before the start of the Great War, were eyeing up new colonies and seeing how far they could test the strength of new alliances.

In early 1900, the War Department wrote to the Home Office expressing concerns about the disposal of convicts from Borstal in the event of a major emergency, such as a threatened invasion. Being so close to the first line of defence (Fort Borstal), in the event of an emergency, the prison would need to evacuate its 450 convicts, but the concern was that there was no suitable place in the district to secure them, and there was no suggestion that they be released in any instance. Lord Lansdowne, then Secretary of State for War, suggested that at any point an invasion became imminent, that prison authorities must evacuate all convicts to other districts less likely to be affected by military operations.

Given that prisons at the time were at or above capacity, it was lucky that no such invasion threat occurred, as from the record there is no evidence that any safe locations were ever identified.

The end?

In January 1902, it was announced that Borstal as a convict prison was to close, with the chain of fortifications the convicts were constructing having been practically completed [27]. Later that year, the War Office officially objected to the closing of the convict prison, citing an old agreement, and insisting that at least one hundred prisoners remain to be engaged on the Forts [28]. This is probably why the convict prison did not officially close until 1906, and there was a period of crossover with the convicts and juvenile-adults incarcerated in separate accommodation.

But this was not going to be the end of Borstal completely. Plans were already underway to transform it into a new type of reformatory for boys, as we'll look at in the next Chapter.

CHAPTER 2
BORSTAL INSTITUTION

It was reported as early as May 1901 that Borstal as a convict prison was to undergo a transformation. The general feeling of unease amongst the convict population following the embarrassing escape of Soar and King (see Chapter 6) probably only hastened such.

Background and the management of youth offending

Under the Youthful Offenders Act (1854) children under the age of 16 found guilty of crimes could be sent to prison for a maximum of fourteen days. They would then be moved to a Reformatory School for anywhere between two and five years. These schools were run by voluntary groups but with state aid. Punishment was doled out which included military drills and hard labour. In 1861, a further Act was passed which included children under the age of 14.

The Industrial School Act (1866) introduced establishments for orphans, children of convicts and dangerous children. They would receive a basic education and industrial or agricultural training. By the 1870s, there were 50 industrial schools and 65 reformatory schools, but despite this, juveniles were still being sent to prison well into the 1890s.

In 1895, the report on the findings of the Gladstone Committee were published, being the last major committee on the running of prisons in the nineteenth century. Chaired by Herbert Gladstone, the committee aimed to design a prison system which concentrated on reforming the individual rather than punishing them and had a greater understanding of the type of criminal and his needs. The Prison Act (1898) represented the manifestation of most of the committee's findings. The Act led to the abolition of unproductive labour (such as the treadmill and the crank), stipulated that prisoners were to work together, learn trades and have better access to books [20]. Isolation could not be imposed for periods longer than a month.

The *Gladstone Report* acknowledged that young offenders needed a different type of treatment in prison, and that they should not be mixed with older prisoners. It also criticised the long-term incumbent chair of the Prison Commission, Sir Edmund Du Cane, who resigned as a result. In his place the Home Secretary appointed Evelyn Ruggles-Brise, whose main task was implementing the recommendations of the Report, and thus the Borstal system was born.

In researching potential reformation of juvenile detention, Ruggles-Brise in 1897 travelled to the United States, to study their more advanced juvenile reformatory movement. He visited the Elmira Reformatory in New York state, run by the "father of prison reform" Zebulon Brockway. He was said to be favourably impressed by what he saw, and upon returning started an experiment at Pentonville, Wandsworth, and Wormwood Scrubs with juvenile offenders between the ages of 16 and 21 [29].

"The elaborate system of moral, physical, and industrial training of these prisoners, the enthusiasm which dominated the work, the elaborate machinery for supervision of parole, all these things, if stripped of their extravagances, satisfied me that a real, human effort was being made in these States for the rehabilitation of the youthful criminal." [30]

On 30 April 1900, the Home Secretary met with a group representing reformatory and industrial schools, to consider, amongst other things, a request to extend the age at which "youthful offenders" could be committed to the reformatories.

Mr. Ritchie told the delegation that, regarding these offenders who were too old for reformatory or industrial schools, the Government was going to deal with them in a similar way, stating that Borstal Prison was going to be converted into one where the reformatory principles would be applied to boys. Accommodation for one hundred boys would be available within 12 months. The

Government had drafted a bill for dealing with these offenders which Mr. Ritchie hoped would be introduced within that Parliamentary session [31]. That bill was laid before the House on 26 June 1901.

The Borstal system

In 1901, Ruggles-Brise was instrumental in forming the London Prison Visitors Association, a society which he authorised to help monitor the prisoners taking part in his experiment. In October, the secretary of the charity, William Haldane Porter, wrote to newspapers to make the public aware of the society's mission, to ask for funds and volunteers. Initially, they would interview prisoners who had been selected as suitable for the experiment whilst in custody, to ascertain the details of their case, and to prepare the ground for their treatment upon release. After discharge they would endeavour to *"obtain a good influence over him and to help him back to honest habits of life and work by every possible means"* [32]. The society would later become the Borstal Association, and each month they would visit Borstal to interview those due for discharge in the following month, with a view to providing them appropriate aftercare upon release. They were funded with a £100 annual bursary from the treasury, supplemented by an income of around £400-£500 of annual subscriptions from generous friends.

The Society was first involved in an experiment at Bedford Prison, where they supervised all the criminals discharged from the "special class" of juvenile-adults and selected from those who had been sentenced in London to a year's hard labour (or over). At Bedford, these boys were kept away from adult prisoners, but they received no aftercare on discharge. The plan for Borstal was to take those juvenile-adults from Bedford who had long sentences but also provide the aftercare.

Having established an association, next Ruggles-Brise needed to establish the system. The objective was to cease the "evil habits" by treating the prisoner as an individual, mentally, morally, and physically. He added physical drill, gymnastics, vocational and educational training to the regime. As well as this were introduced a system of grades and rewards to encourage good conduct, which although small and trivial, were designed to encourage a spirit of healthy emulation and inspire self-respect.

At this time, the system was not recognised by an Act of Parliament, so he had to act within the constraints of existing penal law. This meant he could only transfer existing young prisoners of 16-21 who had been sentenced to imprisonment for at least six months. It soon became apparent that the system required time to work, the best results to be seen after 12 months, but this was a longer sentence than the law permitted.

When the first 100 juvenile-adults were moved to Borstal in 1901, cells were created for them by amalgamating pairs of the convicts' sleeping berths into rooms measuring 9ft x 9ft x 7ft 6in high (2.7 x 2.7 x 2.3m). More cells were formed after the convict prison officially closed in 1906.

An inmate in his cell (two berths made into one. 1902. Note the tidy bed pack!
Howard League / University of Warwick (MSS.16A/7/23/1/21a-b)

In 1906, after five or so years' experience of his experiment, Ruggles-Brise had established the key principles of the Borstal system.

- That boys of 16-21 be sentenced for not less than one year and not more than three.

- That they receive physical labour and skilled trades.
- That they receive education and are supported by both the Schoolmaster and the Chaplain.
- That upon discharge they are supported into lodgings and employment by the Borstal Association.

He addressed the Secretary of State asking for the law to be changed to support the system, and thanks to agreement by both the Secretary of State and the Chancellor of the Exchequer, the principles passed into law under the Prevention of Crime Act 1908.

By June 1908, there was accommodation for 256 boys. There were also workshops, a school room, and a farm. Borstal as a prison especially benefited from the system because of its land and the facilities afforded to it whilst it was a convict prison. Boys could immediately be put to work in the fields surrounding the prison, as well as in the number of workshops that were already present, such as woodworking, metal-working and tailoring. After completing physical work, they would undertake educational study in the classroom.

Inmates in the school room. 1902. Education was as important as labour at Borstal. Howard League / University of Warwick (MSS.16A/7/23/1/23a-b)

Inmates carrying out field work. 1902. This looks like a cabbage and potato harvest.
Howard League / University of Warwick (MSS.16A/7/23/1/9a-b)

Inmates in a metal workshop. 1902.
Howard League / University of Warwick (MSS.16A/7/23/1/14a-b)

Inmates at the blacksmith's forges. 1902.
Howard League / University of Warwick (MSS.16A/7/23/1/16a-b)

Inmates in a woodworking shop. 1902.
Howard League / University of Warwick (MSS.16A/7/23/1/19)

The Chapel. 1902. One of three buildings from the original Borstal Convict Prison which remain today, although with a different layout. Note the gas lamps and the separate areas of worship for staff and prisoners. A warder stands in a booth where he would watch out for prisoners misbehaving. Photograph taken from the mezzanine choir loft, accessed from stairs at the rear of the building (under the clock tower), since removed.
Howard League / University of Warwick (MSS.16A/7/23/1/12)

More inmates working out in the field. 1902.
Howard League / University of Warwick (MSS.16A/7/23/1/8a-c)

A view of the gardens outside the Prison. 1902. In the foreground is some sort of metal barrel with 'C.P.', the initials of Convict Prison, and the broad arrow marking it as British Government property. In the background above the perimeter wall, you can see what appears to be the prisoner escape signal (as below).
Howard League / University of Warwick (MSS.16A/7/23/1/4a-b)

Left. A newspaper excerpt of a photograph showing two officers stood next to a signal on the roof of a building at Borstal. It was used to signal at a distance that a prisoner had made their escape. I have not been able to determine how it operates exactly, but it looks as though the circle is normally hollow but is either closed with coloured plates in the 'escape' aspect or illuminated. [33].

Inmates completing physical drill on the parade ground. 1902.
Howard League / University of Warwick (MSS.16A/7/23/1/2a-c)

Another position in physical drill. 1902.
Howard League / University of Warwick (MSS.16A/7/23/1/3a-c)

Deconstruction and reconstruction

In April 1908, work commenced on demolishing the old halls and building new cellblocks, with much of the work undertaken by the inmates themselves.

Boys starting to demolish one of the original accommodation halls. National Justice Museum.

The four new wings were detached, two-storeyed, and orientated north-south. They were arranged in parallel pairs on either side of a central area containing the former convicts' chapel. The penal aspects of the buildings were kept to a minimum, and the cell windows were designed to be domestic in appearance. Three wings, B, C and D, were built with open landings and contained 100 cells, each measuring 10ft 6in x 7ft x 9ft high (3.2 x 2.1 x 2.7m), the first finished in 1909, the second in 1910 and the third in 1911. The fourth wing, A Wing, was completed in 1912-13. It had classrooms and dining rooms on the ground floor and dormitories either side of a corridor on the first floor and was used for running a more enhanced regime for boys. Other new buildings included a gymnasium, bathhouse, and gatehouse, completed in 1909.

Boys working on constructing what is now B Wing, c.1910. National Justice Museum.

More wing construction work, c.1910. National Justice Museum.

Boys under watchful guard, with construction nearing completion. National Justice Museum.

An inside view of wing construction work. The first-floor cells were serviced by a narrow landing in what is known as an atrium style. National Justice Museum.

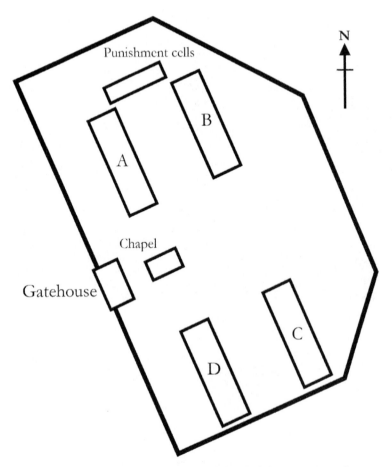

A plan of the layout of the wings following the 1908-1913 reconstruction work

Whilst prisoners had worked outside of the prison before, the external perimeter hadn't previously been extended to make a more secure area, until now. In 1915, construction began of a large workshop (orientated north to south), just north of the previous perimeter wall, and this workshop still exists today, having in the past been the Prison's laundry. At the same time, a single storey building was constructed just north of the Gatehouse, which was later used as a Visits Hall, and two stores' buildings, one later used as a Gymnasium, the other as a training centre.

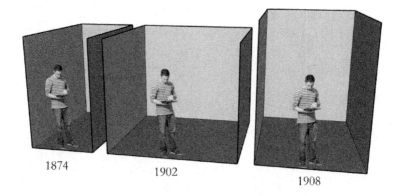

1874

1902

1908

A scaled comparison of the cell sizes. On the left is the original convict berth. In the middle is the first juvenile-adult cells (amalgamated from two berths). And on the right is the purpose-built cell in the wings built between 1908 and 1911.

The operation of the early system

The Borstal system was described by Alexander Paterson, a Commissioner of Prisons:

"At the heart of the system is the recognition of the individuality of the lad. They are not the raw recruits of a conscript army, to be arranged neatly in rows according to their physical stature, to be swung rhythmically in a mass across the parade ground to the beat of a drum. Each is a different and a difficult problem. It is because they must be handled individually with sympathy, firmness and discernment that those who handle them must be rare individuals. The strength or weakness of the Borstal system lies in the strength or weakness of the Borstal staff."

Borstal never wanted to be described as a Prison. Borstal was an "educational training school" but where liberty was curtailed more severely than at a public school. Underneath the Governor were house-masters, not warders, and chief officers and instructors.

Borstal boys could move through a grade system via promotion from "Browns" to "Blues":

Grade I – from conviction (for three months)
Grade II – three months
Grade III – three months
Probation – three months.

Ordinary dress or "Browns" for all newly received prisoners consisted of a brown cap, jacket, and puttees (a cloth wrap covering for the lower leg from the ankle to the knee, sometimes known as a leg wrap). Through good conduct, boys could rise to special dress or "Blues". They could also fall to hodden grey, the colour which indicated the penal grade.

Boys leaving a workshop in Browns. National Justice Museum.

By the end of this time, they would have passed from basic labour, laundry, and farming to a specific trade party. They could take up carpentry, gardening, baking, painting, tailoring and shoemaking.

Probation was a true test of the making of the Borstal boy, where he would receive a change of status and a change of clothing. By this time, he would be expected to show a high degree of perseverance and trustworthiness, and he would demonstrate this by passing into blue dress.

Becoming a leader, he would need to pass through another three grades as a Blue before the chance of being discharged. Privileges that could be won by Blues included smoking, working without supervision, staying up later at night, house amenities, greater levels of trust, and attendance at certain clubs.

In certain cases, Blues were able to wear discharge dress (a suit) and attend instruction outside the Institution at the local technical school for three of four nights a week. The average number of boys attending outside school was fifteen in 1934. The entire system at Borstal was designed toward sending him out into the world as a civilian who could appreciate the value of a trade, the pleasures of exercise and reading, and with a real knowledge of the trust and confidence that can exist between fellow-men – a far cry from the lives of crime that Borstal boys endured prior to their commitment [34].

Until 1924, the officers at Borstal wore the same or similar uniform to that in force when it was a Convict Prison. But after much protest from both staff and the visiting committee, the Prison Commission on 1st June 1924 issued an order relaxing the dress code of officers from uniform to "mufti" (own clothes), to *be regarded as masters in a reformatory establishment rather than discipline officers in a penal establishment.* By the next year, officers had begun to complain about the quality of the civilian clothing that they had been issued under contract, and on 20th May 1925 it was decided instead to pay an allowance in lieu of uniform at £5:7:1 (around £240 today).

The organisation in 1934

There were five houses, four of which were named after previous Governors [35]. The fifth house was called New House. A special sort of training took place in New House, a form of induction, for three months before getting passed on to the main houses. The organisation of the houses was as follows:

BLAKE	RICH	ECCLES	WINDER	NEW
Yellow	Green	Red	Blue	White
90 boys	85 boys	88 boys	88 boys	60 boys
Housemaster	Housemaster Assistant Housemaster	Housemaster Assistant Housemaster	Housemaster	Assistant Housemaster in charge

Blake House was initially going to be named Brise, after the founder of the Borstal system, but the Prison Commissioners felt that it would be better named after the Governor in command when the first boys were admitted [36].

The boys in each house were divided into groups under senior boys known as group leaders. There were also inter-group competitions held for cleanliness and good conduct.

The whole establishment consisted of five Housemasters, five Assistant Housemasters, a part-time Medical Officer, a steward and six clerks, two engineers, five matrons, one chief officer, five principal officers, sixty officers, and about twenty-five temporary staff, night patrols, farm hands, instructors, and stokers.

The canteen system

At Borstal, the canteen pay rates per week in 1934 were:

2d. (a week)	For the first three months.
4½d.	For the next three months.
7d.	For the next three months.
9d.	For the next three months.

The items that the boys could buy with their "badge money" included cigarettes, sweets, matches, razor blades, and hair oil. The Steward purchased stock for the whole institution, and then each Housemaster would stock £5 worth of goods in his "shop" at convenient times, the boys then spending their badge money within their credit limits. Twopence would buy five cigarettes, but they were not allowed more than ten cigarettes a week (although hoarding did happen and was punished).

The profits from the canteen went into the canteen fund, which helped to buy various games for the Houses as well as to pay for repairs to billiard tables, etc.

First Aid classes

As well as the standard education system, boys were able to complete basic first aid training. After being taught bandaging and stretcher work by the hospital officers, and attending lectures by the medical officer, they would be examined by a doctor appointed by the Medical Association. If they passed, they would receive a certificate from the St. John's Ambulance association. A year later there was the option to try for a more advanced certificate, but because of the sentence lengths at Borstal, most of these were issued after the boys had been discharged.

The library

The library at Borstal in 1934 was reported to have contained an impressive number of books, which was added to each year by means of a capitation grant from the Home Office. The Governor and the Housemasters together chose the books to be added. There was a central library for both technical and fiction books – technical books had to remain there, but other books could be changed once or twice a week by each House, to keep the books circulating.

The Phoenix

One particularly interesting feature at the time was the existence of a quarterly newspaper at Borstal. From July 1923 to October 1924 this was known as the *Borstalian* and from January 1925 onward this was known as the *Phoenix*. It dealt with various modern topics, and to the curious reader, gave the impression that the boys at Borstal kept to a high intellectual standard.

The newspaper was edited by a Housemaster, who had under him a boy from each house (not necessarily a Blue) as a sub-editor, whose job it was to collect material for publication – only material relating to Borstal was accepted. Topics included the Editorial, House Notes, poems, fables, notes on the inter-house reading and reciting competitions, rugby cup, association cup, the Chapel, and letters to the Editor.

Published four times a year, Special Grades could purchase a copy for 2d., paid out of their badge money. Around 9 out of 10 boys would send their copies home or to relatives once they had read it. This served another purpose, in that it informed parents and families that the Institution was more like a school than it was a Prison.

It was so popular that it was officially registered as a newspaper and listed in Willing's Press Guide [37].

Phoenix, 1925 (as *Borstalian*, 1923). Jan., Apl., July, Oct. 3d. Sub. 1s. 3d. per ann. H.M. Borstal Institution, Rochester. (Tel. Chatham 73).

The daily routine

The routine at Borstal Institution was much less regimented than it was as a Convict Prison:

TIME	TASKS
05:45	Rise and wash
06:15 – 06:45	Drill
06:50	Breakfast
07:40	Prayers
08:00 – 12:00	Work
12:00 – 13:00	Lunch
13:00 – 17:00	Work
17:00	Tea
18:00 – 19:45	Private study, reading, hobby classes, school, etc.
19:45 – 20:30	Recreation and games
20:30	Supper
21:00 – 21:30	Bed

Education

Learning took place in classrooms in the evening between 6 and 8pm, except for the illiterate. The subjects included map-reading, seamanship, English, mathematics, geography, history, and hobbies, like rug-making and stool-making – officers and Housemasters would often lecture on these subjects and receive pay for their overtime work.

A seamanship class demonstrating sailing techniques. National Justice Museum.

But earlier on in 1917, the situation surrounding learning at

Borstal was in a dire state. An inspection for the Commission in May found a series of failings, including [38]:

- That too much time was given to promising cases to the detriment of "the backward".
- That the tutors were not devoting sufficient time for teaching – in fact, one of the tutors, a Mr. Gwilliam, was not actually present in the Prison for the hours they were contracted, thus breaching the requirement of 7 hours daily attendance of the Civil Service Regulations.

But progress was made, and in 1929 it was reported that *"the best comment on the progress in education generally in the last few years is in the attitude of the lads themselves, which has passed from undisguised antagonism through guarded indifference to its present state of genuine enthusiasm."* [39]

Employment and labour

On arrival at Borstal, a boy would automatically go on to the cleaners or scrubbers party, where he would remain for about three months when new arrivals came. From there he might go on to the laundry, the institution cleaners, or the market gardeners, all located within the walls. After a few months, he would then go to a labour party outside the walls – farm work, roadworks, or general labouring.

By this time, he would have been interviewed by his Housemaster as to whether he wanted to take up any of the trades taught at the Institution. If he chose to, he would be placed on the waiting list, but remain in his labouring party until he was senior enough to fill a vacancy in the trade party. Many opportunities were therefore given for the boys to learn a trade to find gainful employment after discharge from Borstal. By 1934, trades on offer included:

- Cooking, in the central kitchen
- Fitting and turning
- Blacksmithing
- Boot-making and repairing
- Carpentry and stool-making
- Farming, on the 250 acres of land.

Food

Prison food wasn't all bread and water – this punishment had ceased long before Borstal started taking juvenile adults. Below is the meal list in place from 23rd June 1930 (breakfast, lunch, and tea).

	WEEK 1	WEEK 2	WEEK 3	WEEK 4
MON	Porridge Salt Beef & Dumplings Margarine	Porridge Soup Margarine	Porridge Salt Beef & Dumplings Jam	Porridge Soup Margarine
TUE	Preserved Meat Roast Beef Margarine	Sausage Shepherd's Pie Currant Loaf	Bacon Meat Pie Margarine	Bacon Roast Beef Margarine
WED	Bacon Sea Pie Jam	Preserved Meat Roast Mutton Margarine	Sausage Roast Mutton Margarine	Preserved Meat Hot Pot Currant Loaf
THU	Sausage Meat Pie Margarine	Bacon Sea Pie Margarine	Porridge Beef & Treacle Pudding Margarine	Porridge Sea Pie Margarine
FRI	Porridge Irish Stew Currant Loaf	Brawn Hot Pot Jam	Brawn Sea Pie Currant Loaf	Sausage Shepherd's Pie Margarine
SAT	Brawn Beef & Treacle Pudding Margarine	Porridge Meat Pudding Margarine	Bacon Irish Stew Margarine	Bacon Meat Pudding Jam
SUN	Bacon Cold Beef & Pickles Cake & Margarine	Bacon Preserved Meat & Pickles Cake & Margarine	Preserved Meat Cold Beef & Pickles Cake & Margarine	Brawn Preserved Meat & Pickles Cake & Margarine

The kitchen and bakehouse at Borstal, year unknown. National Justice Museum.

One of the dining halls, year unknown. National Justice Museum.

Boys received three meals a day – breakfast, dinner, and tea, and whilst there was generally standardised procurement in the borstals of most foodstuffs, the diet for boys at Borstal was supplemented by the vast quantity of vegetables, including potatoes, that they cultivated in the fields surrounding the prison.

In March 1937, the Commission gave Borstal permission to provide extra food for boys who went to early morning physical training which took place before breakfast – this was ½ pint of cocoa and 2oz. bread (or a similar amount of oatmeal biscuits).

Wartime rationing would later affect the amount of food available to Borstal boys. In May 1944, their official allowance was as follows:

ARTICLE OF FOOD		AMOUNT	
		lb.	oz.
Bread	daily	1	8
Meat Preserved	weekly	-	4
Meat Fresh (value)	weekly		10d
Bacon	weekly	-	4
Potatoes (cooked)	daily	unlimited	
Jam, syrup, treacle	weekly	-	4
Vegetables fresh (cooked)	weekly	1	8
Vegetables root (cooked)	weekly	-	14
Vegetables dried (uncooked)	weekly	-	9
Sugar	weekly	-	8
Oatmeal	weekly	1	5
Rice -or-	weekly	-	3½
Barley	weekly	-	7
Flour	weekly	-	14
Dried fruit	weekly	-	4
Milk	weekly	up to 7 pts	
Margarine	weekly	-	6
Fish (up to)	weekly	-	10
Tea	weekly	-	1
Cocoa	weekly	-	8
Cheese	weekly	-	2

Games and recreation

There were lots of opportunities for sporting endeavours at Borstal. There were cups for both football and rugby, and various other games. Sports included cricket, boxing, athletics, gymnastics, and indoor games. There were also inter-House leagues, which fostered a sporting spirit among the boys, but there were never individual prizes because the emphasis was on everyone to improve the achievement of the group.

The Borstal football team, year unknown. National Justice Museum.

A stage existed in the Gymnasium where occasionally plays produced by the Houses were performed in the evening. This would often include a singsong which involved the audience.

Eccles Camp, 1929. National Justice Museum.

An annual camp was available for the Blues, which was much awaited by both the boys and the staff. In 1933, at the Annual

Housemasters' Conference for Borstal Institutions, attendees bemoaned having to scrimp and scrape for the expenses to cover the costs for camp each year, the grants for such being cut dramatically in 1932. They agreed it was an essential part of Borstal training, and a useful incentive for the boys to work toward.

A demonstration of boys' gymnastic abilities, c.1920s. National Justice Museum.

Boys posing with crossed batons, c.1920s. National Justice Museum.

The long-reaching hand of the Association

The Borstal system was described as a collaboration between the Home Office and "benevolent persons" for the purposes of saving youths and young men who, were such a system not in place, would be lost to the adult criminal justice system. By the year 1894, no fewer than 16,000 young men were passing through the prison system each year. Many were eventually released from prison with virtually no prospects and with less support than they had when they were first incarcerated [40].

Between March 1906 and March 1907, 186 young prisoners passed through the hands of the Borstal Association, and only a small number of these had either returned to prison or not taken on the work they were found. The majority, according to the Association's reports, were "doing well", with some emigrating, some sent to sea, and for most, work was found near to their home. Wherever the young men ended up, the Borstal Association did not admonish their responsibility for them until they firmly found themselves on their feet.

The Borstal Association started its work on the prisoner well before he was due for discharge. They would visit him inside Borstal to interview him about his prospects. After learning about his previous life and associates, they would contact his family and friends to determine how much home support was available to him, and keep an eye out for possible employers, with a view to arranging for him to start work as soon as possible upon release. If they could not find him employment, they would arrange lodgings for him until a job was found. Even once he had secure employment, the Association would continue to visit him to ensure he remained on the right path and is not at risk of being incarcerated again.

Some of the Association's aftercare records are held by the National Justice Museum in Nottingham. I am privileged to be able to reproduce summaries of two records, as examples of the lengths that the Association took to keep boys diverted from a life of crime.

Morris was sentenced to twelve months on 5th October 1909 for housebreaking and larceny, having two previous convictions for the same.

MORRIS, D.

The Governor recorded that he could not be trusted. The Chaplain said that he was one of the worst types, full of sneaking tricks. The Medical Officer stated he was short-sighted.

On a visit to his home prior to discharge, the agent reported that there was a danger of bad company, and that he shouldn't return there. His stepmother thought he was rather weak mentally.

He wanted to go to sea, but the Association didn't think him worth the expenditure, and his family said he could earn a living tailoring. After speaking with the Chaplain, it was agreed to send him to sea.

On 4th October 1910 he was discharged from Borstal, and by 6th October he was sailing on the steamship Villa Boog bound for Galati and Braila (now Romania) as a trimmer earning £2.

The Association had contact with his stepmother and father whilst he sailed, until his ship arrived at Glasgow on 28 December.

The Board of Trade contacted the Association in January 1911 stating that Morris had died. In further correspondence, the Board stated that he jumped overboard on 18th October, and that his stepmother and a girl who was said to be his fiancée were at the Board offices and very distressed.

Manley was sentenced to twelve months for housebreaking. Both the Governor and the Chaplain had a favourable opinion of him, expecting him to do well. The Chaplain stated he had wanted to return to his employer, and when he was seen by the Association he wanted to work on buildings or with horses.

MANLEY, FREDERICK

When an agent visited his home in June 1907, they found his mother had run away, the house was very dirty with chickens in the kitchen, and it was a rough area. He was discharged from Borstal in August 1907 to his home address, but the Association advised he ought not stay there and put him up in lodgings. After a few attempts, he was finally found work, where his foreman reported favourably. He was supplied with Sunday clothes. In September he was seen at work, where other lads said he was a drinker, but for a while all reports came back favourably, even after returning home to live.

In early January 1908 he started new work but had been put off and was trying to join the Army. In February, word reached the Association that he had been sentenced to another twelve months in Wormwood Scrubs.

In his final contact in June 1912, after being released from Prison, he asked the Association to be able to emigrate.

The impact of war

As early as 1938, with tensions in Europe rising, the Government was already making plans for managing domestics affairs in the event of the outbreak of war. Prison Commission correspondence early on shows that when hostilities started, 'A' Hall at Wormwood Scrubs Prison in London would be made available within 24 hours for use by MI5 (the military intelligence department), expanding to the rest of the prison shortly after [41]. The closed women's prison, Shepton Mallet, was also designated for use by the Public Records Office, for storage of sensitive and historically important documents well away from London.

It appears that several government ministries were vying for the use of prison accommodation during hostilities, as evidenced in correspondence, the Commission appeared to get quite irate with requests, and understandably so. No firm decision had yet been made about what would happen to prison populations after the outbreak of war, so it was impractical for them to pledge that any accommodation could be made available at certain stages.

On 26th January 1939, the Prison Commission wrote to Eric de Normann at HM Office of Works outlining plans to evacuate certain prisons to reduce the potential loss of life from gas or bomb attacks. Brixton, Pentonville, and Wormwood Scrubs in London, as well as Portsmouth, would be fully evacuated. In addition, Birmingham, Holloway, Hull, Leeds, Liverpool, Manchester, Wandsworth, and Borstal would be partly evacuated. However, the Office of Works were still keen to find alternative accommodation, and evacuated prisons seemed ideal.

In March 1939, the Prison Commission published a set of Emergency Orders marked 'SECRET', to be read by the Governor, Deputy Governor, and a few senior staff at each prison, before being secured under seal in the Governor's safe [42].

The orders applied to all or to specific prisons and would be activated upon Governors receiving a coded telegram. On receiving SEAL DETAIN, which would have been sent soon before war broke out, Governors would start detaining certain suspects and enemy aliens arrested by the Police, as well as reporting the presence of any enemy aliens in their prisons to the Police, to MI5 (at Box 500), and the Commission.

On receipt of SEAL PROCEED, or outbreak of hostilities, the rest of the orders came into action. Immediately, all Borstal inmates who had served six months or more of their sentence would be released on licence. The Borstal Association could not operate the same as it could pre-war, but lads were still advised to make regular contact with the Association, and to enlist in the Armed Forces as soon as possible (specific arrangements were made so as not to disallow Borstal lads from serving).

The day afterwards, Borstal would transfer 12 officers to Portland prison. These officers and their families would meet the Camp Hill and Portland escort at Southampton and proceed by rail. Twenty inmates would be retained to maintain the farm, and for domestic services. The remaining inmates not licenced under the Paragraph 8 order would be transferred to Feltham under escort of a housemaster who would also remain at Feltham. Another 10 officers, one nursing sister, and five matrons would also be transferred to Feltham borstal institution. Later, when their services could be spared, thirteen officers were transferred to Maidstone to ultimately replace Officer Reservists.

On the outbreak of war in September 1939, for whatever reason, the Institution was completely evacuated and placed into maintenance mode. But less than a month later, thirty 'star' class convicts were transferred in from Maidstone Prison to keep the farm working. For this to take place, the Principal Secretary of State made a declaration on 11th October 1939 that the Borstal Institution was to be designated a Prison, under the Prison Acts of 1865 and 1877 (this declaration would later be revoked on 10th April 1940).

These men were moved into one wing, Blake House, next to which an air raid shelter had been constructed. The farm and agricultural land were tended to, the heating and hot water systems were maintained, and the external telephones were kept manned at all hours.

A naval connection

In December 1939, the Civil Lord of the Admiralty, Captain Hudson, met the Home Office to request the use of the Prison for the accommodation of naval personnel based at Chatham. The Home Office wrote back on 27th December rejecting this request, citing a report from the Commissioners which stated that Borstal was not actually empty as the Admiralty had presumed (now that 34 Maidstone convicts were tending the farm). The Home Office also raised issues with borstal accommodation nationally, that not all Institutions had the same security levels, and as Borstal was deemed the most secure at the time, there may have been a need to reoccupy it at short notice, as the only reserve Institution [43].

At the time, the farmland covered nearly 200 acres, of which potatoes covered 8 acres, cattle fodder (turnips, etc.) 10 acres, cereals

83 acres, and pasture 88 acres, and between 8 and 10 lead dairy cows.

The Admiralty were apparently not happy with the rebuttal. On 3rd January 1940, the First Lord of the Admiralty, none other than Winston Churchill, wrote a memo to the War Cabinet requesting the use of the Institution again.

CHATHAM BARRACKS.

I AM sorry to trouble my colleagues with what may seem a small matter, but it is one of great importance to the Navy.

There is at present very serious overcrowding at our Naval Barracks. As regards Chatham, the only solution possible appears to be to take over the Borstal Institution at Rochester which was evacuated at the beginning of the war. It would be ideal from our point of view, having accommodation for about 1,000 with parade and recreation grounds attached. The only alternative is a disused workhouse, which is verminous and will require big expense to adapt it to our purposes. Apart from the discomfort to the men, the danger of an epidemic breaking out in the present crowded barracks is considerable.

We have accordingly consulted the Home Office, who inform us that owing to evacuation and other causes the number of Institutions available for Borstal purposes has been reduced from eight to rather less than five, and the total nominal accommodation from some 2,200 to some 1,100. Although the actual number of Borstal inmates is at present little more than 800, they estimate that [they] may have to provide during the next financial year for 1,200. They also state that the Rochester Institution is one which provides a fair degree of security, and that as it is their only reserve Institution, they may be forced to reoccupy it in spite of its situation in a very vulnerable area. There are at present thirty-four convicts from Maidstone there who are long-term prisoners being given a little more freedom before being released.

It will be seen, therefore, that the question upon which I seek a decision is whether the pressing needs of the Navy should not over-ride the desire of the Home Office to keep a Reserve Prison, for which they may never use.

It will always be possible for the Navy to evacuate the Institution should circumstances make its use by the Home Office essential at some future date.

W. S. C

Admiralty, S.W.1,
January 3, 1940.

The Home Office, having had sight of this memo before it was brought to Cabinet, continued to make ever weakening representations to the Admiralty, before eventually admitting that they would have no option but to allow the Navy use of part of the site. The Prison would retain Blake House (with its shelter), an adjacent workshop and the Special Cells, all of which would be separated from the rest of the site by a wooden fence. The 8 Party Gate provided means of access to the farms outside for the convicts that remained. The agreement was based on a review after 6 months, that the whole Institution would be evacuated within a fortnight if required for prison purposes, and that the Admiralty would not alter the buildings they occupied.

As well as buildings within the boundary wall, the Admiralty also made use of four official residences outside (most probably the houses of the Governor, the Deputy Governor, the Medical Officer, and the Chaplain), an area referred to as HMS "Hawke".

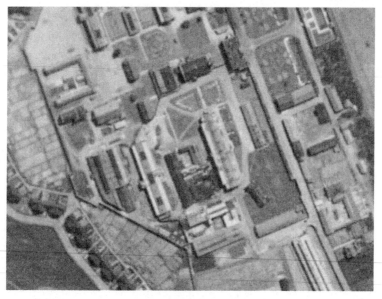

The area fenced off for the use by the Prison. Historic England, with permission.

At the end of March 1940, the borstal population nationally had risen (as the courts were still operating as per peacetime) and the Prison Commission decided it was necessary to cease the use of Borstal as accommodation for prisoners, and re-open it as an

Institution for 80 boys. An order revoking the Prison declaration was made on 10th April 1940. The Admiralty still retained the use of the rest of the Institution.

In June 1941, after the bombing of Portland and the change of use of Feltham, there were again increasing population pressures. The Prison Commission concluded that they would have to relinquish the Admiralty of some of their accommodation, starting with Rich House (the hall adjacent to Blake).

By May 1942, the national population had increased even further, and the Commission were forced to ask the Admiralty for the entirety of the Institution back. After much toing and froing, the Commission agreed that the Admiralty be left Eccles House, the parade ground and the four residences outside, and they remained there until 1945, when the Home Office had to go directly to the First Lord of the Admiralty to evict them! The Navy finally left on 1st July 1945, nearly two months after the end of hostilities in Europe.

Wartime damage

It is difficult to quantify the level of damage caused by German air raids during the war, because of the restrictions of reporting in the press. However, it is well-known that the Medway towns suffered a heavy share of bombing attacks during air raids between 1940-41.

In August 1940, the first bombs had started to drop on Borstal, but with no damage (unlike at Portland, where the same series of attacks killed four borstal boys, injured another five, and took a House out of action). Bombs fell again in September, this time the boiler house, farm, and several other buildings were hit, but thankfully not severely so, and without casualties.

In January 1943, Borstal was hit by two high explosive bombs and several incendiary bombs, but with no damage caused and no casualties.

It was the shrapnel from one of these bomb attacks which caused damage to a prison building which can still be seen today. On the north-eastern aspect of Blake House (now the Activities building) there is a pattern of damage to the brickwork on the first storey, which resulted from a bomb hit on the complex of workshops and buildings between Blake and Hawke houses.

*An aerial photograph taken by the RAF in June 1942, with Fort Borstal in the lower right.
Historic England, with permission.*

Whilst the buildings and people who stayed at Borstal were mostly unaffected by War, others were not. Many staff were mobilised into the Armed Forces and saw their fair share of conflict in Europe and afar.

Borstal Housemaster Alexander John Severs Mackenzie, originally from Yorkshire, was present at the 1938 Annual Housemasters' Conference, the last before the outbreak of war. He was mobilised during the War and saw action in North Africa and the Middle East with the Royal Signals, and in 1942 was Adjutant of 50th (Northumbrian) Divisional Signals Regiment. In October 1945, he was returning from Cairo to London with his wife Dorothy (who was a Wren) when the Short Stirling they were flying on crashed outside Rennes, France, killing all 26 on board. They are buried side by side at Rennes Eastern Cemetery.

The headstone of Lt. Col. Mackenzie at Rennes. Photograph by Derek Burgess, with permission.

CHAPTER 3
BEYOND THE BORSTAL

During the 1930s, Borstal (and other borstal institutions) appeared to have achieved remarkable success, with claims to have rehabilitated around 70% of trainees that passed through their gates. However, by the early 1970s, that success was no longer sustained, with around 70% of trainees who left borstals being reconvicted within two years of their release [44]. The basic system had varied little in forty years, yet British and indeed world society and social attitudes had altered massively.

In the early 1970s, it held 312 trainees: 232 in Nelson, Rodney, and Hawke houses, 68 in Blake house (which had dormitory accommodation), and 12 in a special unit accommodating outworkers selected to work for local firms. The progressive house system had been abandoned, and new arrivals from Wormwood Scrubs were allocated based on personality traits identified through staff judgment: those characterised as 'aggressive' went to Nelson, the 'immature and inadequate' to Rodney, the 'disturbed' to Hawke, and a random group, subject to certain qualifications, to Blake.

Several problems affected the Establishment as a whole. In August 1969, 5 trainees had assaulted an officer in an attempt to abscond. In January 1970, 3 trainees died after they set a fire in a barricaded cell. Borstal violence was regularly reported in the press, with a local newspaper running with the headline '*BORSTAL VIOLENCE – give us the facts*', and the News of the World leading with *'End the fear of Coshville demands a judge'* in March 1971.

The failings of the borstal system were becoming more apparent, and it was thrown into the spotlight in the late 1970s by the banning of the Roy Minton and Alan Clarke play *Scum*. Two years later, it was remade as a film, which despite being toned down from its original, remained highly controversial in its depiction of violence and bullying, not only amongst inmates, but also by the prison warders. It also showed elements that had never been depicted in the past, such as the large number of black inmates who were subject to racism from both inmates and staff [45].

From Borstal to a youth custody centre

Within two years of the film's cinema release, the Criminal Justice Act 1982 officially abolished the Borstal system in the United Kingdom, replacing them with youth custody centres, and this was when Borstal, as an Establishment, was first named Rochester.

But the prison had already been evolving. As a result of changes in the prison population nationally, in 1971 construction began of a new 120-bed remand centre, by prisoners, outside the perimeter wall. Once built, this was named Cookham Wood Prison, and was also furnished with many officers' quarters on the new Cookham Wood Road, but before it had even opened it changed use to a female prison. As part of the same development, but undertaken by contractors, a 60-bed unit was built on the site of the former New House, later to be known as C Wing, and was opened by Lord Colville on 3rd April 1973. The old hospital was demolished and replaced with a new Healthcare centre. Later developments in the 1970s included a new wing attached to the Healthcare centre and a new Education block on the old parade ground.

This was another period of flux – officers were reportedly overburdened, having to look after 270 boys with levels of violence on the increase. It was estimated that serious trouble broke out at least twice a day, with reports of violent incidents double that of previous years [46]. Even after the abolition of borstals and a name change, HM Youth Custody Centre Rochester was in a dual role position where it accommodated both youths and adults on remand.

C Wing, built in 1971.

The Special Cells, later the Segregation Unit, prior to a new roof being installed at the beginning of the 21ˢᵗ Century, looking virtually the same as when it was built in 1878.

The Gate, taken from just outside the old swimming pool. Note the portico (which was removed in 2006) and flagpole on the gatehouse roof.

The Chapel and the Memorial Garden

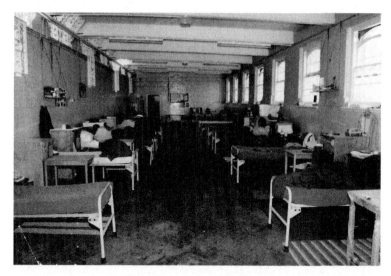

One of the dormitories in Blake house.

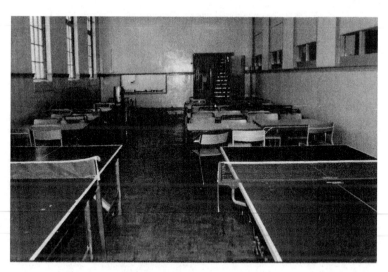

A dining and association room in Blake house.

The Education Block, not long after its construction in the 1970s. National Justice Museum.

A boat building class taken in the Education block. 1970s. National Justice Museum.

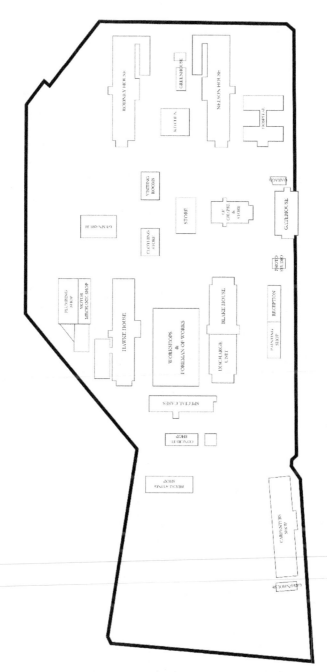

A plan of the Prison from 1967, based on a drawing held by the Medway Archives.

A young offenders' institute

In September 1987, it was announced by the Home Office that Rochester was to change its role to a local prison and take on a full range of adult offenders. The aim was to make better use of prison accommodation by taking pressure off other overcrowded jails in the South East, with the conversion due to start in April 1988. At the time of the announcement, Rochester was designed to hold 357 prisoners, but only 275 young offenders were housed there, along with several adult remand prisoners [47].

In 1988, the prison's role changed again, and it was designated a Young Offenders Institute, as HMYOI Rochester.

The move to a Prison

By April 1989, the conversion to HM Prison Rochester was almost complete, with the last of the young people being moved out. Three wings would be used to house youths on remand, and two would be used for low-risk adults. The prison held 281 men, of which 61 were adults, but the capacity was 440 [48].

In 1991, in the shadow of the Strangeways riots the previous year, it was reported that just three officers oversaw 100 prisoners on the remand wing at Rochester. The chair of the Prison Officers Association (POA) branch at the time blamed staff shortages on the lack of funding by the Government. Training courses for staff away from the Prison had also stopped. This was the start of a period where there were virtually no new staff recruited at Rochester, after the *Fresh Start* programme which phased out overtime for prison officers and moved them all to a 39-hour week [49].

Detainee Centre

The Prison Service announced in June 1994 that Rochester would become one of five specially designed centres to hold immigration detainees, providing 200 spaces in two renovated accommodation units (D and E Wings). At the time of the announcement, detainees were held in 41 different locations, and the idea was to try and rationalise resources and allow immigration staff to apply themselves more effectively. The changes were due to be completed by September that year [50]. In July, members of the

Medway branch of Youth Against Racism in Europe held a protest outside the Prison's gate, voicing their opposition to the plans. Another protest took place in December, but neither had any effect as Rochester had already been holding detainees on D Wing since July.

In January 1995, E Wing opened after refurbishment, allowing the detainee capacity to rise to 200, and the site was designated as HM Detainee Centre Rochester. Concerns had been raised by numerous organisations including Amnesty International, forcing the Prison Service to invite Medway News to look at the centre for themselves. Translators were available, although staff tried to communicate as much as possible with simple English and hand signals. The Deputy Governor reported that staff never forgot that the detainees were not criminals, so the treatment and mindset was completely different.

The typical daily routine for a detainee was:

TIME	TASKS
08:00	Wake up call. Detainees use their own washing facilities and go to breakfast
08:45	Clean rooms – earn 30p per day
09:00 – 12:00	Opportunity to go to education classes, exercise in the gym or outside, or entertain visitors
12:00 – 13:15	Time alone in cells
13:15	Lunch
14:00 – 17:00	Education, exercise, or visits
17:45	Main meal
18:30 – 20:00	Association and telephone calls
20:00 – 08:00	Locked in cells.

The prison kitchen tried its hardest to cater for the various cultural and religious needs, but quickly discovered that detainees wanted traditional British meals. One African detainee remarked at the time: *"If I had wanted African food then I would have stayed there."* [51]

Groups protesting the locking up of asylum seekers continued both outside the Prison and in other locations for months afterward. In September, outside Rochester Cathedral, Father Bert White resigned as Chaplain of the Prison, slamming the system. The acting Governor at the time said: *"We are paid to lock people up. I work for the Prison Service, and it is not up to me to make moral decisions on whether it is right or wrong."* [52] Detainees, reportedly around 50 illegal immigrants, held their own passive protest on 1st August 1995, after being asked to sign compacts giving them enhanced conditions [53].

A 1993 inspection by HM Inspectorate of Prisons (HMIP) criticised staff morale, the regime for young offenders and the poor state of repair of some of the buildings. In 1994, the Home Office had threatened market testing and privatisation of the Prison after branding it one of the worst 21 in the country, and members of the Prison Officers Association (POA) had even passed a vote of no confidence in management. But a later inspection in 1996 found that a new Governor had brought sweeping changes throughout the Establishment.

By this time, the role of the prison had expanded to cover immigration detainees, sex offenders, young offenders, and prisoners on a resettlement programme. Inspectors praised the high level of commitment and enthusiasm showed by staff. Detainees were also reportedly upset at the loss of Sky TV, which was removed at the end of 1995 after the provider reportedly priced itself out of the market. Allegedly detainees were prepared to pay back some of their wages to get the privilege back, but it was illegal to charge prisoners for special facilities [54].

Tensions in the jail continued into 1998, with immigration detainees going on hunger strike amid growing staff shortages. Local press reported that staff were working under difficult conditions and still waiting for back pay they were owed. The local POA branch chair said that staff shortages meant that inevitably detainees had to be locked up longer, which led to their dissatisfaction. The Prison Service stated that more staff were in the process of being transferred in, to alleviate the concerns [55]. Towards the end of 1999, ten staff would later transfer to Rochester after the closure of HMP Aldington, outside Ashford.

Back to young offenders

On 18th October 2001, young offenders on B Wing started a riot, and held a prisoner officer hostage by overpowering him and locking him in a cell, after beating him with a pool cue. The riot started at 19:40 on the wing, which held 63 young offenders; specialist, riot-trained Tornado teams stormed the unit and regained control at 04:00 the following morning. Significant damage was caused to the wing. Three men were found guilty of prison mutiny and false imprisonment after a three-month hearing in December 2002 [56].

Rochester was subject to a re-role in the middle of January 2002, with its remit changing to young men under the age of 21 and was designated HMYOI Rochester. This followed an announcement by the Home Secretary in October 2001 that detainees held solely under the powers of the Immigration Act would no longer be held in prisons. The detainees from Rochester were transferred to Immigration Removal Centres (IRCs) or to the dedicated immigration detention facilities at HMP Haslar and HMP Lindholme, which would in February also be designated as IRCs [57].

Expansion

In October 2006, because of population pressures (79,843 nationally, leaving only 125 spaces), the Home Office implemented Operation Safeguard – the use of police cells to hold prisoners who could not be accommodated in prison establishments. The contingency operates under the Imprisonment (Temporary Provisions) Act 1980, which allows prisoners remanded or sentenced to prison by the courts to be held in police cells for one night, except over weekends or bank holidays when the period could be longer. It ceased temporarily at the end of December 2006 but was reinstated mid-January 2007.

The Home Office was compelled to give serious consideration to increasing the availability of prison spaces. Plans were laid to convert the disused Connaught Barracks in Dover into an open prison to house around 200 Category D prisoners for around five years, but these were eventually thrown out [58]. Another location would be needed.

Rochester was blessed with lots of land, some of which was already within its secure perimeter, including a sports field, but in the time since it was first built, the village around it had also expanded. Local properties surrounding the prison wall which were formerly officers' quarters had since been sold off and were now private residences.

The Chapel and clock tower, around the beginning of the 21ˢᵗ century.

On 23ʳᵈ March 2007, the Home Office submitted a planning application to Medway Council for a 300-place prison extension within the secure perimeter, taking the capacity from 392 to 700. But local residents were incensed because building work already appeared to have started without permission. They said that they had seen cranes and lorries on the site, with trees being felled and roads widened to gain access, and a new car park already laid. As a result of this, the local authority wrote to the Home Office expressing their concern that work on the proposed five two-storey accommodation blocks, sports centre, and other facilities appeared to have commenced, despite the planning application only just being received [59].

As a result of the local authority's intervention, the Prison Service halted building work on 3rd April, until a detailed planning application had been registered, consulted on, and decided [60]. Local consultations were made with residents nearby, and a revised planning application was submitted in late May [61]. The local authority postponed a planned meeting to decide on the application in August, in order to have further discussions with the newly formed Ministry of Justice. Campaigners and the local MP opposed the plans and sent nearly 150 letters of objection, citing traffic and environmental concerns [62].

Permission was finally granted on 9th November 2007 and construction of the expanded site was finished in June 2008. Whilst the original plan had been for five new wings, taking into consideration some concerns raised by residents, this was reduced to four, with one wing being twice the size. The site plans were redesigned to move wings away from the nearest private residence. The owners of numbers 1 to 28 Sir Evelyn Road were also able to extend their gardens as part of the development. In a nod to the past, the area of the new site closest to these houses was also developed as a market garden for the growing of fresh produce for the prison kitchen. This ensured that the properties would not be directly overlooked.

The accommodation units were designed and built by a partnership of Premier Modular Group, Capita Symonds and Wates Construction. Each wing took three weeks to install, with most of the construction and fitting out taking place at a rapid assembly factory, which could manufacture 40 cells in a week. Despite the quick turnaround, the buildings were all certified as permanent structures [63].

New buildings meant new names, and the decision was made to name the wings after places in Kent – Aylesford, Burham, Chilham, Detling, Eccles, Frinstead, Greatstone, and Headcorn. Initially R Wing was the new Resettlement wing, but this would later be named Ridley Wing.

Bringing in the adults

In June 2011, the prison role changed again, and became joint young offenders and Category C. The new wings had minor refurbishment work completed whilst the new receptions of Category C prisoners trickled in over the next few months. Initially the adults were kept apart from the young offender population, but eventually both cohorts would go on to mix across the site.

The mega-prison that never was

On 22nd March 2017, then Justice Secretary Liz Truss announced that four new mega prisons would be built, at Full Sutton, Hindley, Port Talbot in Wales and at Rochester, as part of a £1.3bn programme to transform the prison estate [64]. In a statement at the time, she said:

"We cannot hope to reduce reoffending until we build prisons that are places of reform where hard work and self-improvement flourish. Outdated prisons, with dark corridors and cramped conditions, will not help offenders turn their back on crime – nor do they provide our professional and dedicated prison officers with the right tools or environment to do their job effectively."

The planned demolition and rebuilding of Rochester Prison was strongly supported by both the local MP and local councillor, but was opposed by residents, who had joined the *Community Action on Prison Expansion* group. The news also had a massive impact on staff, some of whom took advantage of an opportunity to transfer to the newly built HMP Berwyn in North Wales, taking their families with them.

An outline planning application submitted by the Ministry of Justice to Medway Council on 10th May 2017 showed a provisional plan to increase the Prison perimeter as far as the boundary with Cookham Wood to the south and the brow of the hill facing the Medway valley to the west. Buildings in the existing area of the perimeter would be a maximum of two storeys high so as not to affect surrounding properties, but those in the newly extended area to the west were going to be up to four storeys high.

The Prison was due to close in September 2017, with staff moved to other local jails and prisoners transferred, and a skeleton staffing left on site whilst the demolition and construction took place. Detailed site surveys were undertaken by contractors, including traffic counts on Maidstone Road and Sir Evelyn Road.

But by the end of July, the redevelopment paused. The Ministry of Justice announced on 24th July 2017 that the prison expansion and modernisation plan had been postponed until 2019, due to a sharp increase in the national prison population. This caused another upset amongst staff, who were now kept in a period of limbo, with some staff already having transferred and others planning to do so.

Two years passed, and there was no further mention of the redevelopment taking place. The Covid-19 pandemic greatly affected the operation of the justice system nationally, meaning that fewer people were being committed to prison by the courts, so there was no longer a justification for such a widescale prison expansion project. The redevelopment plan has never officially been rescinded by the Ministry of Justice, but it is not expected that a budget exists anymore to fund the work.

The prison today

Today, Rochester holds around 695 men in single and double cells, some of which have showers, and all have toilets.

As a resettlement prison, they offer a wide range of vocational training, work opportunities, and offending behaviour programmes. Vocational training includes painting and decorating, bricklaying, carpentry, stonemasonry, plastering, tiling, welding, construction skills, and catering. There are opportunities for education, including English and Maths, IT, and distance learning [65].

In 2023, work began on constructing new accommodation "pods" to increase the prison's operational capacity, following similar projects to improve capacity at other jails during the Covid-19 pandemic. These single-occupancy pods, which look like small portacabins, are constructed, and fully fitted off-site, and then craned into position where the services are then connected. It is hoped that these pods will provide accommodation for another 50 prisoners [66].

The Rochester Crest

In 2018, the Prison unveiled a new crest to cement its identity.

The north-western quadrant features a golden lion on a red background, a symbol of the old City of Rochester, as is the golden cross on a red background in the south-eastern quadrant. The key and the portcullis represent security.

The current crest of HM Prison Rochester.

CHAPTER 4
THE FORTS AND THE RAILWAY

We can't look at the history of Borstal without paying attention to the primary reason for the prison's existence – the construction of the Eastern Defences by convict labour. To do this, we need to go back a bit further and consider the strategic role played by the River Medway and the Dockyard at Chatham.

Chatham started to be used by the Royal Navy as a dockyard in the mid-16th century. There was a gun battery at Gillingham and a blockhouse at Sheerness, but to protect the dockyard more effectively, in 1559 the construction of Upnor Castle began. In 1585 a chain was added from the castle across the Medway to the dockyard opposite. In the 1620s, the dockyard was greatly expanded, and a wall built around it.

After the Dutch sailed up the Medway and attacked Chatham in 1667, two extra gun batteries, Cockham Wood Battery, and Gillingham Battery, were constructed in 1669 as extra defences.

Although approach from the sea was protected, there was a new concern that the French would invade and attack the dockyard from the land. In 1756, a line of fortifications known as the Cumberland Lines commenced around the dockyard and the town of Brompton, around a mile and a half in length. The Townsend and Amherst redoubts were built at either end of the Lines. At the beginning of the 19th century, Amherst was greatly strengthened and became Fort Amherst. The Cumberland Lines were expanded north to cover the larger dockyard and the village of St. Mary's. Around the same time further defences were added – Fort Pitt (1805-1819) on the heights in Chatham and Fort Clarence (1805-1811), a large brick gun-tower to the south of Rochester Castle [67].

Palmerston's Follies

In the late 1850s, there were serious concerns that France might attempt to invade the United Kingdom. The Victorian era had seen great improvements in gunnery and the widespread introduction of steam propulsion in ships. When Henry Temple, 3rd Viscount Palmerston returned to power in 1859, public concern over this naval arms race, combined with Napoleon III's aggressive intervention in the Second Italian War of Independence, allowed him to act on his conviction that Britain's coastal defences were inadequate to prevent invasion if the Royal Navy was lured elsewhere [68].

The *Royal Commission on the Defence of the United Kingdom* was a committee formed in 1859 to enquire into the ability of the United Kingdom to defend itself against an attempted invasion by a foreign power, and to advise the British Government on the remedial action required. In the following year, the Commission's report recommended a huge programme of fortification to defend the country's arsenals and naval bases.

The land defences for the protection of Chatham, known as the Eastern Defences, or the Chatham Ring Fortress, were intended to prevent an enemy force who may have landed at an undefended beach from marching overland and assaulting the dockyard from the rear, or simply bombarding it. Construction did not start until 1875, after the Franco-Prussian War of 1870-71 had removed the threat of French invasion and rendering the forts needless. They would later be known as *Palmerston's Follies*.

Eastern Defences Railway (EDR)

Work on the forts first involved construction of a 1ft 6in / 18-inch gauge (457mm) railway. Built by the Royal Engineers, it originated from a pier on the Medway, with a spur from the gravel pits at Borstal. There were two sidings alongside the wharf and a signal to control train movements. From here, the railway ran in a straight line up the steep slope to the north-western edge of Fort Borstal, passing under Wouldham Road and Nashenden Lane on the way. The railway then passed the eastern edge of the Fort, past the gatehouse of Borstal Prison (where there was a loop, a station, and railway workshops) then south toward Fort Bridgewoods. After Bridgewoods, the railway sharply turned east through Little Delce Wood on to Fort Horsted. Finally, it passed down what is now The Ridgeway, north-east alongside Magpie Hall Road to Fort Luton [4]. Its total length was around 2½ miles of continuous track. By 1909 it had almost entirely vanished [69].

Aerial photograph of the only remaining evidence of the Eastern Defences Railway today – the dark shaded curve is the discolouration of the grass on the line of the former track. © Google Maps and its contributors.

The choice of the 18-inch gauge for the railway was not a free one – the War Department had at its disposal some special 18-inch gauge locomotives which had been constructed for military use, but otherwise gone unused, so their possession decided the question. [70]

Conventional locomotives and wagons could not haul goods up the steep Borstal slope, nor could they usefully be manhandled by convict labour. The solution was what was referred to locally as "the Handysides". Six experimental 18-inch gauge locomotives had been built by Fox, Walker & Co in the spring of 1878. They had a 2-4-2-wheel arrangement and weighed around 8 tons in working order. On the front was a steam-winding crab, and they were fitted with rail clutches. They were initially tested at Woolwich Royal Arsenal, and then the Royal School of Military Engineering in Gillingham, where they ran on short sections incorporating gradients of 1-in-10 and 1-in-11. After being rejected for field use, by 1880 some of the locomotives had been transferred to the Royal Engineers working on Fort Borstal.

A photograph of one of the Handysides. Location and source unknown.

The system as it worked at Borstal involved using a locomotive both as a mobile and a fixed haulage unit. It was coupled to its wagons by a steel wire rope (rather than traditional couplers) wound on a drum mounted horizontally under the footplate. The drum was driven by an auxiliary pair of steam cylinders. In addition, the locomotive (and some of the wagons) was fitted with gripping struts (the Handyside struts) which, on operating a lever, would grip the sides of the running rails, preventing damage to the top rail surface. Any undesired backward movement of the locomotive caused greater downward pressure on the strut, thus making it grip the rail more tightly. Any forward movement of the loco would unlock the gripping struts and allow onward movement up the gradient [71].

The Royal Engineers overseeing the defences work suggested that it was just as well these locomotives never saw war service, because their build presented so many weak points, some of which could only be temporarily remedied in their work at Borstal [70]. The mounting of the crab engine and the need to make such sharp curves (the locomotives could negotiate a 16-foot radius curve at low speed) severely restricted the boiler and tank capacity and interfered with the rigidity of the frame. To get the running gear over the frame sides, the boilers had to be mounted very high in relation to the gauge, giving the locomotives a very unstable appearance. But the actual stability when travelling up to 10mph turned out to be very satisfactory, and the fact that no accidents occurred with one of these locomotives for four years, running on temporary rails with little to no ballast under the sleepers, was testament to the special design of the engines.

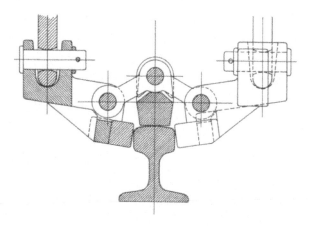

A sectional drawing of Handyside's "Patent Gripping Strutt"

Whilst frequent repairs were necessary to keep the engines under steam, they performed a fair amount of work under rough conditions. Each locomotive, in full work, consumed around 67lbs (just over 30kg) of smokeless Welsh coal and about 61 gallons of water per hour. In a good state of repair, with 140lbs of boiler pressure, the rail traction was nearly one ton, but on average it was difficult to obtain more than two thirds of this power.

For some months, one of these engines was used to haul loads of gravel and other building materials up the incline from Borstal village, graded 1/16 for 500 yards and then 1/25 for a further 1,800 yards, the maximum gross load being around 10 tons. It soon became evident, however, that this was damaging to the locomotive and the practice was discontinued once it became possible to haul up the slope using a winding drum driven by a fixed engine.

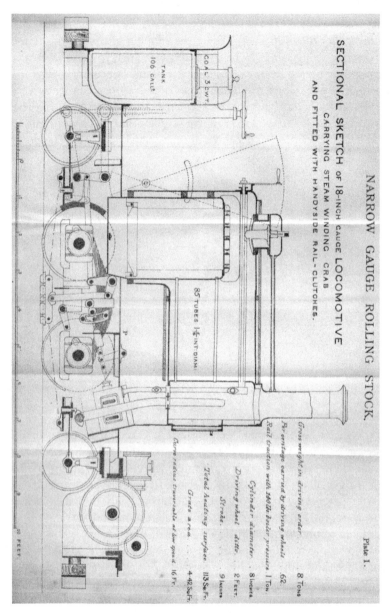

A plate showing the design of the 'Handyside' locomotive [70]

The steam winding crab at the front of the engine was said to be in a practically useless position for hauling loads at the rear, although it was just about possible to pass the winding cable back between the wheels under the locomotive on a straight section of incline. The locomotive would pull its wagons closely until it reached the start of the incline, where it would release the brake on the cable drum and continue up the slope alone. Here the handbrake and gripping struts would be applied, after which the drum would wind the cable back up, slowly hauling up the train of wagons, whose own struts would grip upon halting. The loco would then move up alone again, and the process would continue until the entire train was back on the flat.

The crab engine was successfully put to other uses, however. It found use hauling a gross truckload of 3½ tons up an incline of 1/5 from the excavation of a ditch of one of the forts, and as a shaft pulley to drive concrete mixers and other equipment, by means of a belt system.

It soon became evident that the 'Handysides' could not be relied upon for regular train service, including transport of convicts, so a more efficient type of engine was needed. Attention was directed to an experimental engine designed by Mr. Percival Heywood which had a flexible wheel-base system, but this engine never appears to have been used. Instead, a new engine designed by Major English and constructed at the Vulcan Works was chosen and ran quite successfully. At a gross weight of 10 tons, it could easily haul ten fully loaded convict carriages, weighing about 38 tons, up a gradient of 1 in 50. It had a tractive force about half that of the 'Handysides' but was seen to be far more superior in terms of maintenance.

The pattern of carriage adopted for the transport of convicts was like those in use on the Ffestiniog and Snowdon-Ranger lines in North Wales. Apart from some minor alterations, the design of the carriages never really changed, and they stood the test of many years of constant traffic without serious accident, with a daily passenger freight between Borstal and Horsted at one point exceeding 300 men on each trip.

The prisoners sat back-to-back in the carriages, with a civil guard sat on the outside of each. The original locks were replaced with a chain which was fed along the side of the carriage, through sliding gate bolts and padlocked at its end – this was a much quicker method of securing the carriages. The guard was armed with a small rifle, to be used if a convict tried to escape.

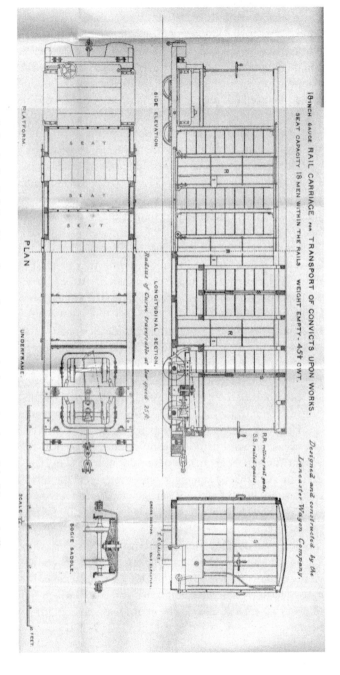

A plate showing the design of the carriages used to convey convicts between the prison and the defence works [70]

The operation of the railway was not entirely flawless. On 17th June 1897, whilst securing the convicts in the carriages, guards noticed that the points within 100 yards of the prison had been tampered with, and had it not been discovered, the train would certainly have been derailed [72]. A month prior, two civil guards named Lobb and Walker were thrown off their seats when the train collided with an empty truck whilst returning to the Prison. They were taken to the infirmary, but the 100 convicts were uninjured [73].

In January the same year a runaway train only avoided causing fatalities because a warder promptly jumped off the train and changed the points in time. It still caused a violent collision, destroying the storekeeper's shed and a railway car used by the Governor. The cause was thought to be a broken coupling, with the worst injury being a convict with a broken leg [74].

For the transport of stores and materials, a number of wagons were built by the Lancaster Wagon Company, arranged for all-round tip, with the bodies being mounted rather high to ensure stability and swivelling upon turntable plates. More than one rolling stock firm confessed they could not see a way to construct end-tipping trucks for the capacity desired, so it is no surprise that the trucks chosen were expensive. The other advantage of the truck design was that they were very convenient for hand shunting by convict labour, without the aid of horses.

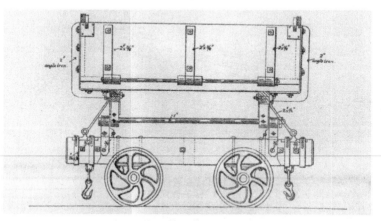

The Lancaster tipping truck [70]

For simple transport of materials without the requirement to tip, a special bogie wagon was employed which had a significantly greater carrying capacity. By lowering the hinged sideboards, it could also be used as a carriage for 26 men, were there not a need for security.

A larger gauge railway, it is agreed, would have been much more economical and would have shortened construction time of the forts if available, but history shows that the railway experiment at Borstal was something of a success.

Fort Borstal

Construction at Borstal started in 1876 and stopped in 1887 when it was thought the forts were no longer needed. It restarted in the early 1890s and was completed in 1895.

It is the only fort in the Chatham Defences to have a caponier for defending the ditch. The caponier is a small outwork of several galleries that juts out from the main work to provide flanking fire to protect the ditch. It also served as the mounting for the drawbridge. There was also a very long counterscarp gallery running along the south section of the ditch. The fort had a main row of casemates at the rear and a main magazine line at the right flank and in a semi-circle out from the casemates were the expense magazines, and above these were six gun emplacements.

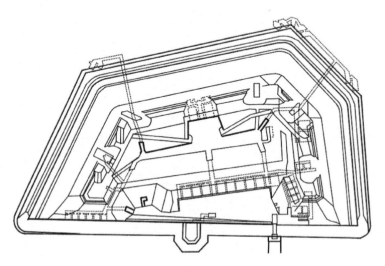

A plan of the layout of Fort Borstal

On 18th October 1878, a convict named Charles Graydon, who was undergoing five years' penal servitude, was killed almost instantaneously when a quantity of chalk fell on him, whilst he was working on the fort [75]. He was buried at St. Margaret's Cemetery, a short distance down the main road from the prison [76]. In July 1879, during excavation work, convicts found the skeleton of a man who, it is supposed, was murdered, and thrown into a hole dug in the woods [77].

During World War II, the fort was a major anti-aircraft battery, having eight QF Mark II 4.5inch anti-aircraft guns in concrete emplacements. Also attached to the fort was an ATS camp. On 15th September 1940, an observer on top of the fort witnessed the shooting down by anti-aircraft fire of six enemy bombers in the space of twenty minutes [78].

After the War, the fort came into the possession of the Borstal Institution, where it was eventually used as a piggery for the farms and gardens department. In the 2000s, the fort was sold off (with a lot of land surrounding the Prison) and is now in private ownership as a residence. It was put up for sale in 2022 with an asking price of £1.5m, but at the time of publishing, has not been sold.

Fort Bridgewoods

The original name for Fort Bridgewoods was Delce Woods Fort, and this appears on a revised Commission Plan of 1872, which also featured a proposal to connect the EDR to Fort Amherst in Chatham. Construction work had begun in 1879. The final layout of Bridgewoods was six-sided, with the longest face to the north and the main works aligned east to west. The gateway was let into the centre of the longest face, at which point the moat was crossed by a rolling drawbridge which could be retracted into a space below the heavily armoured double doors. The name of the fort was painted above the archway of the main gates, with the date of 1889 displayed below the letters VR (representing Victoria Regina).

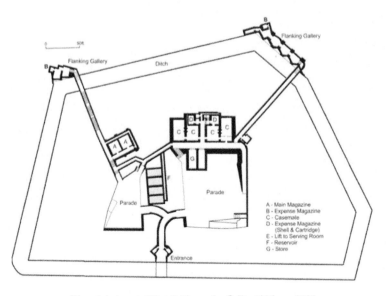

Plan of the layout of Fort Bridgewoods. © David Moore, 2009.

Because of budget restraints and changing ideas of fortifications, no fixed armament was mounted; instead, earthen ramps were built to enable field artillery to fire from the fort's parapet. The fort was a radical departure from traditional design, of earth construction, with a deep dry moat designed to blend in with the line of the land. Its final profile made it difficult to observe from any distance. There were magazines and living quarters under the earthen walls.

During World War I the fort served as barrack accommodation. In 1926, it became a Military Wireless Interception Station, later a "Y" station, intercepting signals and passing them on to Bletchley Park [79]. Hutted accommodation was built in the adjacent East Cookham Wood. Later in WWII, the fort was occupied by the Home Guard who manned light anti-aircraft defences.

In 1953 the fort contained an Anti-Aircraft Operation Room for the Thames and Medway South fixed AA guns sites which remained operational until 1957. The fort was handed over to the Home Office in 1961 and until 1967 it was a Sub Regional Control Centre for the administration of Southeast London after a nuclear attack, known as SRC 5.2. The 1968 Civil Defence cuts axed the Bridgewoods Centre, and the fort was sold to a builder in the late 1970s and the ditch was filled. In 1988 the fort was demolished, and the site now houses a Royal Mail depot.

Fort Horsted

Horsted was the largest of the forts proposed by the Royal Commission. It was originally intended to garrison some 400 men and to mount forty guns. Construction began in 1879 and was finally completed in 1889, after much delay.

The fort was six-sided with a dry ditch, with its angles protected by three counterscarp galleries flanking the three main angles and firing positions flanking the entrance. It originally had a drawbridge over the gorge in front of the entrance, but this was replaced with a fixed bridge after World War I.

It was constructed almost entirely of concrete, topped with chalk and earth with no visible concrete exposed from the outside, except from the gorge or rear of the fort. Although the original plans proposed fixed armament, by its completion it was decided that the fort would not been permanently armed, unless actual threat materialised, and it would then be provided with field artillery.

Troops man a mobile 12-pdr gun, mounted on the back of a lorry, at Fort Horsted, Chatham, 1 December 1940. From the Imperial War Museum.

Between the World Wars and until it was abandoned by the Army in the 1950s, it was used as a depot and stores. It was later used as a car warehouse and a dump for old tyres. It is now a scheduled monument and a business centre.

Fort Luton

Luton was the smallest of the semi-circle forts to the south of Chatham. Its function was to defend the ground between Fort Darland and Fort Horsted that couldn't be covered by their own fire (Darland wasn't built by Borstal labour but was completed around 1899). Construction started in the 1877 and was completed in 1892 (after pausing between 1882 and 1886) when the rolling drawbridge and palisade gates were finished [78].

For thirteen years, the fort was used for summer camps and, on alternate years, the Chatham Siege Trials. The final one in 1907 was the largest in both scope and number of men employed and was in effect a rehearsal for a major war. Significant damage was caused which was repaired in later years, but some is still visible today.

During World War II, the fort became barrack accommodation, and a wooden hutted camp was built nearby. After the war, the fort was abandoned, and later sold to Kent County Council in the early 1960s. Some of the land was used to build Fort Luton Boys Secondary School (now the Victory Academy). The fort was bought in 2012 by a community interest company and now functions as a private hire venue with a small museum attached and opens roughly one weekend a month for visitors and living history events.

A view of Fort Luton as it looks today, courtesy of Wikimedia Commons.

CHAPTER 5
THE GOVERNORS

The position of Governor at Rochester Prison has been held by many people in the last 150 years. There are two sign written wooden boards on display within the Prison on which are artistically written the names of all the Governors from 1901 onwards. I am pleased to reproduce these below. I have attempted to research the names of the Governors prior to this, but there are some gaps in the public record, although Whitaker's Almanacks have been incredibly useful in reducing these gaps. Where research allowed, I have also provided some more details on certain Governors (marked with a † in the table).

BORSTAL CONVICT PRISON

Capt.	A.G. Alexander	1878-1881
Maj.	E.G. Horne	1881-1885
Capt.	G.A. Dawson	1885-1888
Lt. Col.	S.R.B. Partridge	1888-1893
Lt. Col.	H. Plummer	1893-1897
Mr	W.H.O. Russell	1897-1898
Capt.	C. Eardley-Wilmot	1898-1900
Maj.	E. Briscoe	1900-1901
Mr	N.G. Mitchell-Innes †	1901-1902

Mr	A.G. Western	1902-1905
Capt.	F.W.H. Blake †	1905-1907
Maj.	G.R. Elliott	1907-1908
Capt.	W.V. Eccles	1908-1909

N.G. Mitchell-Innes

Before taking over as Governor at Borstal, Norman Gilbert Mitchell-Innes was a Deputy Governor at a gaol in the north of England. But in 1891, he was appointed Colonial Treasurer of the colony of Hong Kong. In 1910 he became the Inspector of Prisons until his death in 1913 [80].

F.W.H. Blake

Latterly Major Frederick Wallace Hastings Blake, in 1926, was prosecuted under the Official Secrets Act for revealing to the Manchester Evening News a confession by the convicted murderer Frederick Bywaters. He was, at this time, retired, and this was the first use of the Official Secrets Act against a senior official. He was fined 250 guineas and costs at the Old Bailey [81].

HM BORSTAL INSTITUTION

Capt.	W.V. Eccles †	1909-1916
Dr	W.H. Winder	1916-1920
Lt. Col.	C.E.F. Rich (DSO) †	1920-1923
Dr	J.C.W. Methven †	1923-1929
Mr	R.L. Bradley	1929-1936
Mr	H. Scott	1936-1938
Mr	J.C. Ransley	1938-1939
Mr	R.D. Fairn †	1942-1945
Comdr.	S.W. Lushington (RN)	1946-1948
Mr	J.C. Ransley	1948-1952
Mr	P.M. Burnett	1952-1958
Maj.	A Sanderson (MC)	1958-1962
Mr	G.W. Fowler †	1962-1966
Mr	N.C. Honey	1966-1969
Mr	D.F. Dennis	1969-1972
Mr	S.A. Bester	1972-1977

| Mr | W.J. Cooper | 1978-1981 |
| Mr | J.S. Shulman | 1981-1983 |

Capt. William Vernon Eccles

Capt. William Vernon Eccles served as Governor from 1908 until 1916, when he died suddenly in service. Previously he had been Deputy Governor at Borstal for around a decade and had overseen the official conversion of the Prison to the Borstal Institution following the Prevention of Crime Act 1908. His name was given to what was previously C Wing, this would later be renamed Rodney House after 1945, and is now called D Wing.

Lt. Col. C.E.F. Rich (DSO)

Lt. Col. Charles Edwin Frederick Rich, Governor between 1920 and 1923 wrote a book entitled *Recollections of a Prison Governor*, in which he described Sir Evelyn Ruggles-Brise (see Chapter 8) as *"an absolute sahib, yet clever and autocrat, accustomed to make up his mind and then sweep all obstacles out of the way of his will."*

In 1923, Rich organised the Institution into houses, with each having a house-master – these firstly were Mr. Butler (the Chaplain), Mr. Leavey, Mr. Hair and Major Grew, his Deputy Governor. Each house had several monitors and contained boys in different stages of their training. At the end of each week, marks were given for conduct and efficiency, and the house which came top got an extra cigarette or another small token of recognition.

The four houses were named after the four Governors who had up until then run the Establishment as a Borstal – Blake, Eccles, Winder, and Rich [82], although why Major Elliott was not included is not clear from the historical record.

Dr. J.C.W. Methven

"We hope in time to get Borstal traditions at least as equal to those of Eton and Harrow" said Methven at a conference of magistrates in Blackpool in 1928. When jokingly reported in the Australian press, they expected future lawyers to wear the badge of the Borstal Old Boys' Association [83]. He was later promoted to oversee Borstal Institutions for the Prison Commission [84].

Mr. R.D. Fairn

Whilst Richard Duncan Fairn governed Borstal during the perils of wartime, he had the rather enviable situation of managing Borstal whilst it had one of its lowest inmate populations, and the fewest number of buildings to maintain.

He was later promoted to Commissioner of Prisons and a Director of Prison Administration between 1952 and 1963. In 1959 he was chairman of a committee on detention camps in Kenya during the Mau Mau Rebellion (or Kenya Emergency). He had already reported on the state of jails in other parts of the Empire, including in British Guiana. Between 1964 and 1967 he was assistant under-secretary of state at the Home Office.

He would later write papers on prisons and penal reform, and in 1962 delivered the Eleanor Rathbone Memorial Lecture entitled *The Disinherited Prisoner*. Fairn died in April 1986.

Mr. G.W. Fowler

Gordon William Fowler was born in 1923. Joining the Army in 1941, he was a subaltern in the 10th Royal Tank Regiment, when he was crushed by a tank on a landing craft during a training exercise, losing his left arm and right leg.

In 1946 he joined the Prison Service, and became a housemaster at Borstal, but his qualities as a trainer were quickly recognised and he was posted to the Imperial Prison Service Training College at Wakefield. In 1962 he was promoted to Governor at Borstal, which he was not entirely happy about, but in 1967 he was personally appointed by the Home Secretary to govern Wormwood Scrubs.

Later he would be promoted to Chief Inspector of Prisons before it became an independent role. Fowler was made a Companion of the Order of the Bath before his retirement in 1982. After that he worked on the Parole Board, and as chairman of the Butler Trust.

Whilst on a lecture tour to the USA, his artificial foot became detached, immobilising him for three days whilst it was repaired. Asked by the Home Office to account for his lack of activity, his reply started: "There was I at midnight in Grand Central Station, New York, sitting on a bench, footloose and fancy free..." He died in 1999.

HM YOUTH CUSTODY CENTRE ROCHESTER

| Mr | J.S. Shulman | 1983-1987 |
| Mr | M. Manning † | 1987-1988 |

Mr. M. Manning

Malcolm Manning served his final year in the Prison Service as Governor of Rochester before he retired. On his retirement day, in a nod to his former role as a Lieutenant Colonel in the Blues and Royals, he was ceremoniously wheeled out of the Prison gate on a wooden horse atop a stores trolley, pulled by four officers!

Governor Manning on his retirement day. National Justice Museum.

HM PRISON ROCHESTER

Mr	D. Wilson	1988-1993
Mr	R.A. Chapman	1993-1999
Mr	A.J. Robson	1999-2000
Mr	J. Robinson	2000-2001

HMP & YOI ROCHESTER

Mr	John Robinson	2001-2002
Ms	Colette Kershaw	2002-2004
Mr	Stephen O'Connell	2004-2006
Mr	John Wilson	2006-2011
Mr	Andy Hudson	2011-2015
Mr	James Carmichael	2016-2018
Mr	Phil Wragg	2018-2018
Mr	Dean Gardiner (MBE)	2018-present

The second sign written wooden board in the Chapel building still has plenty of space for future Governors at Rochester, and it is hoped that the Prison continues long enough to require a third.

CHAPTER 6
NOTABLE EVENTS & FACTS

In this chapter I have tried to capture details or facts about Rochester Prison that don't necessarily fit into the narrative timeline of the first three chapters but have nevertheless popped up during my research. With a history of 150 years, including two world wars, it's no surprise that Rochester has some interesting stories to tell. I hope that a future edition of this book may expand or add to these stories.

Evidence to a committee

In 1895, then Governor, Col. Plummer, gave evidence to the Departmental Committee on Prisons, which later published the Gladstone Report, leading to the 1898 Prison Act.

He had been Governor for 2 years, 4 months, previously he had been the Deputy Governor for 7 years, and the same at Dartmoor for 7 years. He said that accommodation was plentiful, that the convicts were very healthy, and that Borstal did not take convicts with more than five years left to serve of their sentence.

There was no unproductive work except as a punishment, but he stated that he would be sorry to see the crank done away with, because he saw it as being very valuable as a punishment. The crank was in one of the special cells. It was a box filled with sand, to which a handle was fitted, which forced four cups to rotate through the sand. The prisoner would have been ordered to do 6,000-14,400 revolutions over a period of 6 hours. A warder could make the task harder by tightening an adjusting screw on the device, hence the use of 'screws' as slang for prison officers.

Borstal had a 'mark' system, which Plummer was satisfied with. If an officer stopped a mark, the prisoner was 'put down' (listed) to see the Governor the next day to explain himself, and the fact they had to stand in front of the Governor had a good effect on discipline.

He stated that warders' working hours had improved, but that promotion was hopelessly slow. He pushed for a scheme which would allow warders to retire after 26 years' service, a far cry from retiring at 68.

A day out for the family

In 1889, Borstal Convict Prison laid on their first annual summer fete on the cricket ground. Taking place on Saturday 24th August, notwithstanding the showery weather, staff, children, and their parents turned out in apparently huge numbers, for Punch and Judy by the wall and tea served in the library.

At half past one, a procession marched around the quarters up to the Governor's house where they "stopped and gave cheers for the Governor and Deputy Governor, Doctor and the Steward". They continued to the field where the sports events took place. This included throwing the cricket ball, long jump, high jump, flat racing, blind man's buff, tug of war and more [85].

The third annual fete took place on Saturday 11th July 1891, which included Robert Smith's swinging boats, a tent for comic sketches and the usual races and peg pulling. The Chatham Dockyard Police Band being unable to make it were replaced by an "efficient string band" at the last minute. At 4pm, some 400 children and parents sat down to tea, and at 6pm there was a comic sketch by Christy's Minstrel Troupe, with the day ending at 9pm [86].

A great escape

On Thursday 31st May 1900, two convicts named Murgatroyd and King escaped from Borstal, just before finishing work. They made flight in the direction of Wouldham, but armed warders finally captured them and marched them back to the Prison [87]. This was one of a number of escape attempts this year, when morale at Borstal was low, and discussions were being had about the future of the convict prison.

On the densely foggy morning of Friday 30ᵗʰ November 1900, Henry King (the 31ˢᵗ May escape) together with a new accomplice, William Henry Soar, made their escape from Borstal. Soar was an experience gaol-breaker, having escaped Ipswich Prison in 1892, and was only caught after jumping into the River Gipping [88]. Initial reports were that they had stolen a ladder from the prison stores. Armed with crowbars and wearing their broad arrow uniforms, they escaped just before half past seven. Armed prison guards as well as the local police were soon in pursuit [89].

The escapees, as featured in the Illustrated Police News, 15ᵗʰ December 1900.

The next day, plain clothed warders were stationed for miles around the Prison, but there had been no sightings of the pair. On the Sunday, reports were received that a house in Borden (a village just outside Sittingbourne) had been broken into, with clothes, pork, tobacco, jam, and a razor stolen by two men. The local police superintendent followed the men, sure it was the escapees, but they managed to make it the two or so miles to Key Street where two men had broken into another house and stolen more clothes and food. Another potential sighting included a *'woman'* sleeping under a haystack, who when greeted with "hallo there" by a passer-by, responded in a gruff voice and ran away!

On Monday 3rd December, more details were made public. It was thought the two men hid in a prison lavatory on the Friday morning whilst on the way to morning service. They hid under some mattresses that had been stored there. Once the Chapel doors were shut, they climbed up the previously stolen ladder, over the perimeter wall. After getting clear of the wall, they were spotted by a Royal Artillery gunner based at the fort, but he did not raise the alarm because convicts were regularly employed on the fortifications. The men had headed west and were soon lost to the fog. Their escape was not discovered until after the Chapel service had ended.

The search party had been joined by willing local volunteers, but progress was slow because heavy downpours meant any passage away from the main roads was impossible. A reward of £5 was offered for their capture, with police anxious to return them to custody as they were both prolific burglars. The national newspapers reported the story excitedly, expecting them to soon be recaptured.

By Wednesday 5th December, the police had grown weary of the pursuit, with a senior official at Kent Constabulary telling the Evening News, *"I think they are safe to get away now. I don't see how we can expect to catch them."* By this point, a farmhouse in Hollingbourne had been robbed, and every available constable, as well as several amateur detectives, were spreading throughout Kent on the search. But even at this time, suspicions were raised about Soar and King even being in Kent at all – logically at least Soar would have attempted to get to London and then back toward his hometown of Hintlesham, near Ipswich. [90].

On Thursday 6th December, police believed that residents of North Kent were keeping their mouths shut either through fear or misplaced sympathy for the escapees. Searching continued in Blean Woods outside Canterbury, after a mail driver had his horses stopped by two men answering the description of Soar and King and responded in kind by firing four shots toward them [91].

Almost a fortnight after the escape, Mr. E. Brough, president of the Association of Bloodhound Breeders, offered the services of his famous bloodhound, Kickshaw, in the search. Kickshaw had recently taken first prize in the Kennel Club's man-hunting trials.

On Friday 21st December, a rumour was reported that Soar and King were hiding out in Islington, after the hat had been sent around at a "thieves club" with a view to "raising the wind" to provide for them to escape the country [92]. After this, little was reported, until a month later, on 25th January 1901, when a man admitting to being Henry King was arrested on the corner of Euston Road and Hampstead Road in London. He gave the officers no trouble [93].

At the police station, he confessed to being vastly amused by what had appeared in the newspapers about him, particularly the mail coach incident, because he was in London at the time. In fact, both Soar and King were safe in London within a couple of days of their escape. He said that on the way, they had smeared the broad arrows of their uniforms with mud and explained that they were cyclists who had had the misfortune of crashing their bicycles.

William Soar managed to evade capture slightly longer. He was eventually captured in the early hours of Wednesday 17th April, after leaving a house he had been seen living in with a family. Upon interview, he stated that he had arrived at his father's house in Deptford two days after he escaped. After parting company with King, he had been earning an "honest living" at the Victualling Yard at Woolwich Arsenal, and at a shop. He also said that he had overheard several amusing comments about himself whilst on the run, including once in a pub when a man exclaimed *"Why, Soar may be among us now!"* Later that day he was conveyed back to Borstal, to be dealt with [94].

Soar never gave up his criminal ways. After returning to custody and then being released, he would later be jailed again for burglary. He died in London in 1912. King was released from prison in 1904. He featured in the Police Gazette on 20th July 1917 where he featured as an "expert and travelling criminal", so he appears to have maintained his housebreaking tendencies.

The day a strong wind blew

In early February 1877, a severe gale struck the town of Rochester. The Prison site is particularly vulnerable to wind because of its position at the top of the hill, and this vulnerability persists even today. During these particularly strong winds, the corrugated iron roof was pulled from one of the buildings at Borstal and struck a convict, breaking both of his legs. An assistant warder named Shaw was also injured, but less seriously so [95].

An attack by a convict

In October 1893, whilst in a working party, a prisoner named Williams attacked Warder Neale with a shovel, raining down heavy blows. Had he not been dragged away by prisoner Livingstone; the warder might not have survived the attack. Williams was secured with great difficulty and taken to the punishment cells [96].

Murder of a Borstal warder

On a freezing January afternoon in 1920, a police car passed a slow-moving funeral cortege on Maidstone Road in Rochester. The hearse was bearing a man to his final resting place. The police car was heading to Maidstone, transporting the passengers to stand trial for the man's murder.

The dead man was Edward James Adams, a 53-year-old warder from the Borstal Institution. He was known as a kind man and an efficient officer.

This meeting happened five days after Frederick James Cullender (alias Smith) had bludgeoned Adams, snatched his keys, and escaped the Prison, leaving the warder lying in a pool of his own blood.

He had been convicted of theft and shop breaking the previous June and sent to Borstal because of a long list of previous convictions. Institution life had done little to improve his conduct and he had had received several punishments, including the birch.

At the time of the murder, he was awaiting trial for smashing Institution property. Adams had no way of knowing that Smith had spent three days plotting his escape down to the last detail. When he began to create an ear-splitting din in his cell, Adams allowed him outside into the corridor to help with the cleaning.

It was 7pm on Friday 2nd January in the Special Cells, and Smith's plans were going according to schedule. He knew that he had plenty of time before a senior officer's hourly check. And he was sure that the alarm bell had been tampered with so it would not work if anything went wrong.

He crept up behind Adams as he sat at his desk writing his reports and smashed a hard wooden scrubbing brush down on the back of his head. Adams collapsed to the floor. Smith took the prison keys from the inert warder's pouch, grabbed a broom, and made his exit.

Opening the door to the yard, he ran past the schoolhouse (where the current Kitchen stands), scaled the wall with the help of the broom and fled. His escape route took him down the hill to Borstal village, along to Wouldham and then Burham, avoiding the main road and keeping close to the River Medway.

Police throughout the county and London were alerted at 7.30pm, but two Snodland officers, acting on a hunch, cornered Smith, huddled in a cart-shed, at midnight, at Burham Court Farm near the old church.

He went quietly into custody at Malling police station and appeared in court at Rochester Guildhall the following Tuesday. With him in the dock was his fellow inmate, 17-year-old William Ernest Scutt, who had been arrested at Borstal earlier that morning. The two were remanded in custody and were being taken to Maidstone jail when they met the funeral procession coming toward them on its journey from Borstal to St Margaret's Cemetery.

Warder Adams – a former sailor – had been a popular and respected man as the crowds at his funeral testified. The coffin, covered in a Union Jack, was carried on a gun carriage. A firing party and sailors from HMS Pembroke headed the procession and 70 prison warders followed.

The headstone of Edward James Adams at St. Margaret's cemetery in Rochester, 2017. Photograph by Brad Evans, courtesy of Find a Grave (memorial ID: 179269051).

At the inquest, Adams's body was identified by his only son Barry, a civil servant, who lived at his parents' home in Avenue Terrace, Borstal. The governor said that Adams, with 13 years' experience of being a warder, had acted in a highly injudicious manner in allowing Smith out of his cell.

But he had not broken any rules – he had merely acted with indiscretion. The inquest began at 2.30 in the afternoon in the gymnasium at the institution. Seven hours later the coroner wrote down the last words of evidence by candlelight and the jury retired for 22 minutes. The verdict was wilful murder against Smith and the jury asked for its criticism over the lack of regulations governing Borstal discipline to be passed on to the Home Office. [97]

The trial, before Mr Justice Avory, at Kent Assizes, started badly. The hearing had already begun when Scutt's counsel arrived late and asked for a separate trial for his client. After taking advice from prosecuting counsel, Mr Justice Avory turned down the request.

The prosecution took the line that Scutt, who was first on the scene when Smith escaped, could not be innocent else he would have given the alarm. Two kits of civilian clothing had been stolen from a storeroom and a bundle of Scutt's personal belongings had been found in Smith's cell. Smith had claimed that he planned the escape with Scutt, but the other boy strenuously denied this.

The jury retired at 5.15pm and returned to the crowded courtroom just nine minutes later. The unanimous verdict was that Smith was guilty of murder. Scutt was acquitted.

According to tradition, Mr Justice Avory put on the black cap. His lordship said Smith had acted recklessly and had only been concerned about his own escape. The thought that he might have killed the warder had not troubled him. Smith remained impassive as he listened to the words of the death sentence and said nothing as he was led from the court. The execution was fixed for Tuesday 9th March but was postponed when Smith appealed against his sentence. The hearing appeal was refused on 8th March.

It seemed as if the only way out of the condemned cell was by the hangman's noose. But news came the following Saturday, 13th March, that Smith had been granted a reprieve. The Home Secretary notified Smith's mother, who lived in Bermondsey, that the death sentence was to be commuted to life imprisonment.

Throughout all the hearings Smith had maintained that he had not intended to kill. His only statement was made at Rochester Police Station shortly after his arrest when he claimed that he and Scutt had planned to knock Adams out, get his keys and two sets of civilian clothing and escape over the wall.

Only one man will ever know for certain whether the boy intended to kill: Frederick James Cullender, alias Smith.

Adjusting the numbers

In October 1937, the Governor of Borstal, Mr. H. Scott, apparently having spare time on his hands, wrote to the Prison Commission about the superscription on the main gatehouse, drawing their attention to what he perceived as "a mistake in dates".

Above the gate, the words *BORSTAL INSTITUTION* and the year *1908* appear. He argued that as the Governor's journal recorded the official date of opening of the Borstal Institution as 1st August 1909, the date on the gatehouse should be corrected.

In their official response to the Governor, the Commissioners informed him that whilst the Act came into operation in 1909, it was dated 1908, and in fact the prison had been carrying out borstal principles since 1905, and practically the whole population consisted of juvenile adults. He was told by the Commissioners to take no action.

The front aspect of the Old Gatehouse, pictured in 2023.

Interestingly, in the handwritten draft response to his query (not typed in the official response), the Commission noted that it had cost £150 to put the superscription right in 1925 [98]

The superscription above the doors of the Old Gate, pictured in 2023, which has been in place since 1925. There is no record of what the erroneous superscription was.

A downed airman

On Tuesday 8th October 1940, it was cloudy but fair in the South East, with high winds reported. In the morning, two formations of German aircraft approached London. Two hours later, a second attack of 30 aircraft assailed the capital. Fighter Command scrambled 639 sorties to respond. One of these was Sgt Rufus Arthur Ward flying a Spitfire (N3043) out of No. 66 Squadron, based at Gravesend [99].

According to Alan Rose, who was an anti-aircraft gunner at Fort Borstal, Sgt. Ward engaged the enemy above Rochester, but his aircraft was hit by cannon fire from a Messerschmidt Bf109 and its tail was destroyed. Losing altitude, he somehow managed to escape the aircraft, which after flipping, passed Fort Borstal, and crashed near to Valley View Road, alongside the Prison wall [100].

Another eyewitness, Peggy Whamond, reported a great cheer coming up from the gardens when they saw the pilot bale out, and when they saw another plane begin to fly around, they thought it was trying to protect the falling airman. But it soon became apparent that it was another enemy fighter which began firing at him [101].

Sgt. Ward's body could not immediately be recovered because the anti-aircraft guns were still being manned, but as soon as possible he was recovered and removed on a hurdle to the fort. He was buried at Mitcham Road Cemetery in Croydon.

Keeping time

In 2023, a sound returned to the grounds of HMP Rochester that had not been heard for what appears to have been at least twenty years – the hourly striking of the bell in the Chapel clock tower.

Two dials atop the tower, aligned approximately north-east and south-west, now keep accurate time, and one of these is clearly visible from outside the prison wall, near the old gatehouse.

The clock was built by John Thwaites of Clerkenwell in 1798, so predates the construction of the Borstal Convict Prison by some 76 years. It is likely that it was installed somewhere else, before being moved to Borstal.

The movement is of side-by-side birdcage design. It has a going train as well as a striking train, both hand-wound, with a recoil escapement. The pendulum is around 90 inches long and the weights hang 20 feet high, providing a going time of 7-8 days.

Branching out

In late 2022, the Prison planted an area of new woodland as part of the Queen's Green Canopy, a greening initiative to celebrate Her Late Majesty Queen Elizabeth II's Platinum Jubilee.

Over 1,500 native British trees were planted on just over half a hectare of unused grassland to the north of the prison's perimeter wall, to improve the local biodiversity and eventually form a woodland walk area.

This work was supported by a group people on probation as part of the Community Payback scheme in 2023, who undertook a large amount of strimming, mowing, and mulching.

The new woodland area outside of HMP Rochester, shortly after planting in 2022.

CHAPTER 7
BORSTAL MEMORIES

Borstal is a story of people. During the past 150 years, thousands have had interactions with the jail, perhaps as a prisoner confined within, staff passing through the Gate, or as residents in the locality. Here we look at some of those interactions, and some of the personal stories that define Borstal as more than just a prison.

The career criminals

Arthur Harding was born in 1886 in a poor area of London. In later life, he would become one of the more familiar figures in the East End underworld. But before climbing up this criminal ladder, he was one of the first Borstal boys.

On 21st April 1903, he was sentenced to 20 months at North London Sessions, and first served his sentence at Wormwood Scrubs prison. After three months, he and his co-defendant, Peake, were transferred to Borstal, to become what he called "guinea pigs" in Ruggles-Brise's experiment for juvenile delinquents.

When they arrived, some convicts were still serving their sentence at Borstal. Boys were allowed to have more library books and were encouraged to improve their education. There were also schooling facilities for teaching them to read and write.

In his memoirs, written in 1969, Harding said:

"The Governor, a Mr. Western, who was always immaculately dressed, he seemed to wear a different suit every day, he would visit each lad in his cell and talk to him about his future. The Governor was keen to make the new system a success, he continually interviewed every lad, urging them to give of their best to learn a trade so that they would lead useful lives in the community."

Having described himself as a cabinet maker on reception, he was put in the carpenter's shop. Physical training was required every day, which he enjoyed as he felt he had suffered from the close confinement at Wormwood Scrubs. Harding felt that the Borstal system, at least at the start, could not be a success because boys spent the best part of 15 hours a day locked in their cells; staffing difficulties and security issues prevented outside opportunities, with the working day practically ending at 4pm.

Borstal, for him, was not a success, and this perhaps was due to his involvement in its earliest stages. He returned to a life of crime, thinking that Borstal was no different to Scrubs. But he didn't think it all bad:

"Of the success or failure of the first Borstal in the years of infancy, this I can say with truth: it was a step in the right direction. For many years, boys under the age of seventeen had suffered by being imprisoned in dark punishment cells, roughly treated, made to pick oakum."

This story was taken from Harding's autobiography, *My Apprenticeship to Crime*, held by the Bishopsgate Institute.

The making of a professor

Mike Oliver was a sociologist, author, and disability rights activist. He used a wheelchair after breaking his neck in an accident on holiday in 1962.

In 1964, he started teaching at Borstal, under the watchful eye of Peter Antwis, then Head of Education. Peter had heard of Mike's situation and dropped in on him to ask if he might like to help with some literacy work with the young offenders. When Mike said he had no way of getting to Borstal, Peter offered to pick him up.

It turned out that Mike would be replacing another wheelchair user who had left, but for whom workplace adaptations had been made. From individual tutoring he progressed to teaching, studying at night school to prepare for his lessons. It was the new ideas and learning from a sociology module of one of the certificates he earned, that fired his imagination.

Mike credited Peter with getting him the position at Borstal and setting him on his path in life. Leaving Borstal, he started a degree in sociology at the University of Reading but left after a few weeks due to their inadequate support arrangements. He completed his bachelor's degree at the University of Kent, followed by a master's and a doctorate.

He published a book on social work with disabled people in 1983 and went on to become a key advocate of the social model of disability. When he retired, he was Emeritus Professor of Disability Studies at the University of Greenwich, having been the first Professor of Disability Studies in the world. He died on 2nd March 2019.

Mike's daughter Eleanor recalls:

"Borstal gave my dad a new start in life, as well as helping the boys to get a new start. When he first started teaching there in a wheelchair, one of the boys decided to try and attack him. Before dad had his accident, he was 6'5" and a rugby player. My dad got the lad in a headlock and bashed him over the head with one of his books until the officers arrived. He had nothing but respect from them after that."

Recollections of a Borstal officer

Simon Barlow was an officer at Borstal between 1980 and 1988. He wrote a book of his recollections of working there in its final days as a Borstal, which provide a useful insight to those who weren't there at the time.

He recalls trainees being offered courses in motor mechanics, plumbing, bricklaying, carpentry, welding, concrete moulding, and farm work – some of these courses remain today.

"Each morning, they would march from the wings to the parade ground. They would then line up in wing order in front of the orderly officer, the chief officer and the Governor, while the orderly officer took the roll. When the orderly was happy, he would order the boys to form parties. Each party officer would take a position on the parade ground, and his party would form lines in front of him."

In the days when lots of boys would work outside on the farm, and with the M2 motorway being in proximity, the risk of an abscond was high. The procedure for fixed posts, where officers are posted in specific locations to look for an escaped person, were rather more adventurous than today.

"Some fixed posts were outside local pubs, overlooking the M2, which always proved more popular than the local train station or the river crossing. In a 'fixed post' situation, one particular ale house, with a good view of the Medway Valley, would fill up with screws in uniform."

The social club was an incredibly popular part of the Establishment, frequented by staff during their lunch break (as was tradition in days gone by) and a central part of the community, given the large number of officers and their families living in quarters nearby. The downstairs of the building was the social club and the larger function hall, and upstairs was the staff mess, which in later years, despite offering a full-blown lunch for staff at Christmas, got further and further away from the Gatelodge for the staff staple, a bacon butty.! The club in its final guise was known as the Rochwood Staff Club (a contraction of Rochester and Cookham Wood) and was one of the last remaining Prison staff clubs in the country, until it was eventually closed around 2012. It is now a conference and training centre.

He recalls events being run all year round for both staff and their families. A memorable one was a charity fundraiser to collect for the local baby unit, which featured a world record roof tile breaking attempt conducted by a jujitsu club. There was also a rugby match with the Borstal team playing none other than the Harlequins! Sufficed to say, Borstal didn't win.

Several times a year the club committee would run concert nights, however the club came into its own on bonfire night and in the run up to Christmas. The construction of the bonfire would start in earnest in September and would culminate with around £1,000 worth of fireworks on the night of the 5th of November. The Christmas party would see every child receive a gift from an officer who took his role as Father Christmas so seriously, the children were convinced he was the real thing.

Barlow would eventually transfer to the newly built HMP Swaleside (on the Isle of Sheppey), and then to HMP Maidstone in

1994, finally retiring in 2005.

"The first borstal boy that I spoke to in A Wing, Rochester, was also the last prisoner that I saw when I retired from Maidstone Prison in 2005. He had spent all his adult life committing petty crime to fund a drug and alcohol habit."

Barlow's book, *The Self Tapping Screw*, published by Book Guild Publishing (ISBN: 978-1-84624-844-3) in 2013 is a fascinating read.

Life on the farm

As previously mentioned, Borstal benefitted from having a large amount of land surrounding the prison walls, and agriculture was practiced from its original construction and only ceased during the 2008 expansion.

Jon Hayes started working at Borstal in May 1970 as an estate hand, and his good friend John 'Jock' Mollins in June 1972, as a tractor driver and relief cowman. They have many tales about life on the farm at Borstal, probably enough for another book! I will try to cover some of them here.

Loading the haystacks for the winter feeding. National Justice Museum.

In those days, the farm was staffed by a cowman, a pigman, a tractor driver, a foreman, and a manager. There was a small amount of arable farming taking place, with cabbages and potatoes being grown on the lower fields, but this eventually gave way and the farmland which spanned from Borstal village, through Smarts Valley up to Blue Bell Hill was put over to livestock. At its height, the farm had up to 1,000 pigs and a 90 strong dairy herd, as well as the working horses. Initially the herd were Jerseys (for the cream content), but these were eventually replaced with Friesians which produce larger quantities of milk. At one point, there was a memo from HQ sent around the Prisons that stated the Home Office looked after twice as many animals as they did prisoners!

The dairy at Borstal provided all the milk needs for the Prison, but the operation expanded to include Maidstone and then East Sutton Park, with construction of a pasteurisation and packaging facility. There was a fortnightly pork run, where sides of bacon and other pork products were driven around to the Kent prisons to make their deliveries.

Trevor Robinson (Farm Manager), Jon Hayes, a Borstal boy, and Bruce Smith (Cowman), winning an award at the Kent County Show, July 1973.

Both remember ringing the bell on the Gate at 6 o'clock every morning (including at the weekends, when there were always two farm staff working) to collect their inmates, who had been marched there by the two farm party officers after parade, and they would be marched to the farm. A 'cease labour' bell on the Gate would ring later for the inmates to be marched back inside.

When Jon and Jock had started at Borstal, whilst the farm was operational, there was no real offer of qualifications for the boys who worked on the farm. That changed in the 1970s, with proficiency tests and qualifications in animal husbandry being run in conjunction with Hadlow College. The farm also diversified, breeding hybrid pigs for Seghers Hybrids, which would be shipped to all parts of the world.

Borstal cattle crossing the M2, after a photoshoot by the Milk Marketing Board, c. 1970s.

Two films were recorded in part at Borstal, which also involved the farm. *Diamonds*, a 1975 Israeli-American heist film featuring Robert Shaw and Richard Roundtree, shows the outside of the Prison, the Gatehouse and part of the farm buildings (including the conveniently placed milk tanker) in the opening sequence, which really is a blast from the past. *Pig Boy* was a short film drama made by the BBC as part of the 'Scene' series in the early 1990s, which featured Alex Walkinshaw (later of The Bill and Holby City fame), Brian Cox, and Ballykissangel's Tony Doyle. It is about a persistent joyrider who begins a two-year sentence at a young offenders' institute. The prison scenes were filmed at Feltham, but the farm scenes were filmed at Rochester. Jon recalls that the crew descended on a specific day to film a gilt farrowing (a sow in labour). He had given her a prostaglandin injection the previous day, which should induce farrowing about 20 to 30 hours afterwards, but there is absolutely no guarantee it will work. As it happens, the crew set up and began filming the final scene, and she had her litter exactly as they wanted!

Borstal boys ploughing fields with tractors, around the first half of the 20th century.

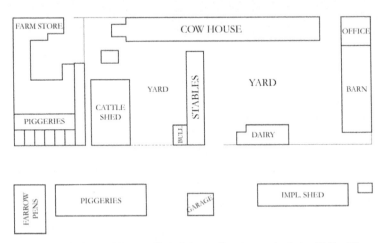

A plan of the farm buildings outside the Prison wall as they were in the late 1960s. These would remain until demolition in 2007. The actual farmland spread over many acres down the escarpment.

Lots of the Borstal lads had come down from London, and some had never seen the countryside. Jock recalls one particular "hard lad" who, when confronted with two boars fighting and told to go in and separate them, quickly scarpered. Another pointed at an animal and asked, *"What's that with the pointy ears?"* – he'd apparently never seen a donkey before.

A soldier based at Fort Borstal feeding a cow.

Whilst the pair have many stories to tell, I'll limit it to two for now. One day the farm received a call from the prison hospital, stating that they had a new inmate who was too heavy for their scales, and asking if they could help. They told the medical officer to bring him out to the farm – they had to get him in the cattle crush to be able to weigh him. On another occasion, when Rochester was a remand centre, a police van arrived at the Gate to bring in a new reception. The prisoner onboard had different plans, and kicked open the back doors, running down the farm lane. Leaping one fence, he continued down, being chased by staff, when he leapt another fence and disappeared. When staff caught up, they saw he had fallen the 20 or so foot drop down into the moat which surrounds Fort Borstal!

One of Borstal's prize-winning Suffolk Punch working horses, being awarded by the actor Oliver Reed (of Oliver! fame), c.1970s.

Hollesley Bay prison used to breed Suffolk Punch working horses for use by all working prisons in England, having until 2002 held the oldest established stud in the world, and Borstal for a long time had three working the farms. Their strength meant they were perfectly suited to ploughing and carting, and Borstal's horses regularly displayed at the Kent County Show, picking up many awards.

Both Jon and Jock look upon their years at Borstal, and then Rochester, as the best years of their lives, and it really does show in speaking with them. Jock had lived in Scotland and had never been to Kent before applying for the job, and he has lived nearby the Prison ever since.

Rolling the fields with the horses after ploughing. National Justice Museum.

The local residents

I posted a request in a local history group, for memories from residents of life near Borstal, and was inundated with messages. Here I have summarised some of these.

"When I was a young man, I attended St. Peter's Methodist Church in Trafalgar Street. Once a month we had about six "Borstal Boys" attend the evening service. After the service, they were invited to go upstairs to our hospitality lounge, where they played table tennis and snooker. I got talking to one of the boys and showed me a picture he had been drawing, it was of a three-masted galleon sailing towards a sunset, it was amazing! Overall, they were ordinary guys who just got on the wrong path. A valuable experience to meet them and to learn from their mistakes." Andrew Boorman

"We lived at the top of Blue Bell Hill and one afternoon some escapees broke into our bungalow. They poured milk over my dad's suits and my parents' bed, and helped themselves to food, as well as throwing clothes and toys all over the place. The second time was late in the evening - we were all in bed and mum heard the rumble of the manual garage doors as they were being rolled back. Without thinking, mum had run out in her nightie and caught the culprits pushing my brother's sports car off the drive. She proceeded to hit them over the head, and they ran off! The police were called, and they said they were looking for some escaped Borstal Boys. Mum got a gentle telling off from the police and all the family for her foolhardy response, but luckily, she came to no harm. I think if it had been now, she would have thought twice." Mavis Brown

"I played football against Borstal boys' teams whilst playing for Riverside FC. We played them at our Esplanade ground and the lads were brought down in a minibus already changed. They would play the game and then get straight back in the minibus back to the Borstal. They had some really good players and I have no memory of any "trouble" - I think they were grateful to be out for a while." Geoff Clark

"My friend and I used to walk from the Tideway in our Sunday best, en-route to Borstal Free Church. We used to walk past the Borstal Institution and see the boys feeding the pigs. We always had a cheeky giggle as we walked past and sometimes, we would get a wolf whistle or two. One day we found a cigarette lighter in the hedge by the prison wall - obviously someone on the outside tried to throw it over to the inmates and it hadn't made it! Two boys absconded from Borstal one day when I worked in the office for Thorns at Rochester Airport - it was exciting watching them out of the windows being pursued by the police. They were caught eventually though." Sandra Church

"I remember it being on the Math School cross country course. You were meant to go round it twice, but if you distracted a certain master enough, he would forget it was your first circuit!" Stuart Smith

I hope that a future edition of this book could be published with new research and even more memories of Borstal, particular from staff throughout the years. If you feel you could contribute to this, I encourage you to contact my publisher.

CHAPTER 8
SIR EVELYN RUGGLES-BRISE

Evelyn John Ruggles-Brise was born in Finchingfield, Essex on 6 December 1857 to Sir Samuel Brise Ruggles-Brise and his wife Marianne (née Bowyer-Smijth). He had three brothers and seven sisters. The family had deep roots in Essex, having been based at Spains Hall since the house was bought by Samuel Ruggles, a clothier, in 1760.

Ruggles-Brise was educated at home and at a private school near Hitchin, before attending Eton from 1869 to 1876 on a scholarship. He read Mods and Greats at Balliol College, Oxford, graduating with a first in 1880. He also played in the college cricket team.

Ruggles-Brise came sixth in the civil service exam and became a clerk in the Home Office in 1880. He was Principal Private Secretary to four Home Secretaries - William Harcourt, Richard Cross, Hugh Childers, and Henry Matthews. The latter appointed him as a Commissioner of Prisons for England and Wales in 1892.

The long-serving chairman of the Prison Commission, Sir Edmund Du Cane, was severely criticised in the report of the Gladstone Commission in 1895 and tendered a hasty resignation. Home Secretary Herbert Asquith appointed Ruggles-Brise in his place. He served as chairman until 1921. His main task was to implement the findings of the *Gladstone report,* and this culminated with the passing into law of the Prison Act 1898.

Portrait of Evelyn Ruggles-Brise, thought to be taken between 1900 and the mid-1920s. From the George Grantham Bain collection at the US Library of Congress.

He travelled to the United States in 1897 to view first-hand the novel methods of managing young adults in custody, visiting the Elmira Reformatory in New York state. On returning, he started an experiment at Bedford Prison which he then moved to a purpose-built unit at Borstal. This later became formalised under the

Prevention of Crime Act 1908 as the "Borstal system".

In 1899, he was awarded a Companion of the Order of the Bath (CB). He was advanced to Knight Commander of the order (KCB) on 26 June 1902 and invested by King Edward VII at Buckingham Palace on 24 October 1902.

He wrote *The English Prison System* in 1921, and *Prison Reform at Home and Abroad* in 1924 – the former was printed by prisoners at Maidstone Prison.

Ruggles-Brise married Jessica Philippa Stonor (née Carew) on 3 September 1914. She died on 29 September 1918. He later married Sheelah Maud Emily Reade on 6 June 1933.

He died of throat cancer in Peaslake in Surrey on 18 August 1935 and was buried at Finchingfield [102]. His pallbearers were six senior prison officers from Wormwood Scrubs, Pentonville, and Wandsworth. The Home Office and the Prison Commissioners were also represented.

The flowers were considerable. They included, besides the official and family bouquets, one bouquet inscribed:

"To the memory of a humane man, Sir Evelyn Ruggles-Brise, K.C.B. He saved me from the cat. Convict 2148".

The national press managed to locate the anonymous convict and interviewed him:

"I was at Parkhurst. I had been sentenced to five years. In those days the prison diet was a starvation one. Everything was weighed down to the last fine ounce. I was one of the ringleaders in a mutiny against the diet. I was sentenced to eighteen strokes with the cat for my part in the affair. Sir Evelyn Ruggles-Brise came down to enquire into the affair. He came to my cell and saw some verses I had written on a slate. He read them. They were:

Prison lashes, cruel slashes,
Human backs they tear:
They never heal but always steal
The virtue ambushed there.

He told me they were good and copied them. Later he got my sentence remitted. He listened to what I had to say about the diet and made many changes.

We got tea instead of skilly, and five ounces of meat instead of weak soup. He was a fine humane man who believed in kindness, in disciplinary methods, not violence."

Adapted from Sir Evelyn Ruggles-Brise: A Memoir of the Founder of Borstal [34].

A caricature of Evelyn Ruggles-Brise by 'Spy' published in Vanity Fair on 10 February 1910.

In June 1925, the Governor at Borstal wrote to Rochester Council suggesting that the name of the road which ran from the Maidstone Road in front of the officers' quarters be named 'Sir Evelyn Road', in his honour. A week later, the change was agreed and confirmed. Sir Evelyn was written to by the Prison Commission to let him know, and he wrote back expressing his gratitude at the mark of recognition of his work.

In the early 20th century, there was an inscription on Borstal's gateway dedicated to Sir Evelyn Ruggles-Brise, which summarises the ideal of Borstal and his dream of its future developments:

"He determined to save the young and careless from wasted life of crime. Through his vision and persistence, a system of repression has been gradually replaced by one of leading and training. We shall remember him as one who believed in his fellow-men."

BIBLIOGRAPHY

[1] Hansard, UK Government, "Hansard - Volume 207: debated on Thursday 15 June 1871," 15 June 1871. [Online]. Available: https://hansard.parliament.uk/Commons/1871-06-15/debates/8aecf6cd-13ff-4062-9ecc-edf59f540b82/NewPrisonNearRochester. [Accessed 9 January 2023].

[2] J. Glover, The Place Names of Kent, Rainham: Meresborough, 1982.

[3] The Church Times, *The Church Times,* London, 1929.

[4] S. Hannington, Out of the Shadows: A History of Borstal Village, Canterbury: Birch Leaf Books, 2016.

[5] Open Domesday, "Borstal - Domesday Book," [Online]. Available: https://opendomesday.org/place/TQ7366/borstal/. [Accessed 9 January 2023].

[6]   Dover Express, "Dover Express," 21 November 1873.

[7]   A. Brodie, J. Croom and J. O. Davies, English Prisons: An Architectural History, Swindon: English Heritage, 2013.

[8]   National Archives, *HO 45/9339/21711 (Home Office),* Kew.

[9]   Rochester Bridge Trust, *RBT Archives.*

[10]   Prison History, "Prison History - Borstal Prison," 2023. [Online]. Available: https://www.prisonhistory.org/prison/borstal-prison/. [Accessed 9 January 2023].

[11]   The Morning Post, "The Morning Post," 21 November 1876.

[12]   The Globe, "The Globe," 4 February 1876.

[13]   P. Higginbotham, "Borstal Convict Prison / HMP Rochester," [Online]. Available: http://www.theprison.org.uk/BorstalCP/. [Accessed 16 January 2023].

[14]   Cambridge Independent Press, 27 November 1875.

[15]   National Archives, *PCOM 7/224 (Prison Commission),* Kew.

[16]   Kentish Mercury, "Kentish Mercury," 17 April 1875.

[17]   T. F. Tannahill, "The influenza epidemic of 1890 at H.M. Convict Prison, Borstal, Rochester," *Glasgow Medical Journal,* vol. XXXIII, 1890.

[18]   Prisons Commission, "Report on the Commissioners of Prisons and the Directors of Convict Prisons 1876," HM

Stationery Office, London, 1877.

[19] J. O'Donovan Rossa, Irish Rebels in English Prisons, New York: D & J Sadler & Co, 1880.

[20] N. R. Storey, Prisons & Prisoners in Victorian Britain, Stroud: The History Press, 2014.

[21] West Midlands Police Museum, "Birmingham City Police Whistle".

[22] Catlemur, "Birching stool National Justice Museum," 15 November 2020. [Online]. Available: https://commons.wikimedia.org/wiki/File:Birching_stool_N ational_Justice_Museum.jpg. [Accessed 23 January 2023].

[23] Home Office, *Memorandum to prisons re: Birches and Cats-o'-nine tails,* National Archives, 1951.

[24] Sheffield & Rotherham Independent, "Sheffield & Rotherham Independent," 13 September 1879.

[25] Shields Daily News, "Borstal Prison Scene Described in Court," 29 June 1904.

[26] Hansard, UK Government, "Hansard - Volume 230: debated on Thursday 22 June 1876," 22 June 1876. [Online]. Available: https://hansard.parliament.uk/Commons/1876-06-22/debates/a1020df7-9963-432e-b27c-a0ecf99bac91/SecondReading. [Accessed 12 January 2023].

[27] The London Echo, "The London Echo," 3 January 1902.

[28] Devon and Exeter Gazette, "Devon and Exeter Gazette," p. 5, 21 June 1902.

[29] N. Cantor, "Measures of Social Defense," *Cornell Law Quarterly,* vol. 22, no. 1, 1936.

[30] E. Ruggles-Brise, The English Prison System, London: Macmillan and Co., Ltd, 1921.

[31] London Evening Standard, "London Evening Standard," 1 May 1901.

[32] Spectator, "Spectator," 26 October 1901.

[33] H. L. Adam, The Story of Crime From the Cradle to the Grave, London: T. Werner Laurie, 1908.

[34] S. Leslie, Sir Evelyn Ruggles-Brise: A Memoir of the Founder of Borstal, London: Butler & Tanner Ltd, 1938.

[35] S. Barman, The English Borstal System, London: P.S. King & Son, Ltd, 1934.

[36] National Archives, *PCOM 7/514 (Prison Commission),* Kew.

[37] Willing Service, Willing's Press Guide, London: Willing Service, 1931, p. 167.

[38] National Archives, *PCOM 7/552 (Prison Commission),* Kew.

[39] Prisons Commission, "Report on the Commissioners of Prisons 1929," HM Stationery Office, London, 1929.

[40] The Westminster Gazette, "The Westminster Gazette," p. 9, 29 July 1907.

[41] National Archives, *PCOM 9/220 (Prison Commission).*

[42]   National Archives, *PCOM 9/2351 (Prison Commission)*, Kew.

[43]   National Archives, *HO 45/23129 (Home Office)*, Kew.

[44]   J. Warder and R. Wilson, "The British Borstal System," *The Journal of Criminal Law and Criminology*, vol. 64, no. 1, pp. 118-127, 1973.

[45]   H. Shore, "Revisiting the Borstal experiment, c. 1902-1982," *Prison Service Journal*, no. 249, pp. 27-33, May 2020.

[46]   Chatham, Rochester & Gillingham News, p. 22, 29 January 1971.

[47]   Chatham Standard, 2 September 1987.

[48]   S. Goldsack, "'Experiment' that lasted 80 years," *Chatham News*, p. 24, 28 April 1989.

[49]   Chatham Standard, p. 6, 5 March 1991.

[50]   Medway News, p. 11, 17 June 1994.

[51]   Medway News, p. 24, 20 January 1995.

[52]   Medway News, p. 3, 15 September 1995.

[53]   A. Roots, "Immigrant inmates stage prison protest," *Medway News*, p. 3, 04 August 1995.

[54]   A. Roots, "Inspectors praise prison reforms," *Medway News*, p. 17, 10 May 1996.

[55]   C. Brown, "Hunger strikes in immigrant centre," *Medway News*, p. 4, 02 October 1998.

[56] BBC, "Three found guilty of prison riot," 04 December 2002. [Online]. Available: http://news.bbc.co.uk/1/hi/england/2543817.stm. [Accessed 02 March 2023].

[57] Hansard, UK Government, "Hansard - Volume 631: debated on Tuesday 5 February 2002," 05 February 2002. [Online]. Available: https://hansard.parliament.uk/Lords/2002-02-05/debates/8df0acff-e36d-4942-8638-85f804787aa1/AsylumSeekersHeldInPrison. [Accessed 02 March 2023].

[58] BBC, "Barracks will become open prison," 21 September 2006. [Online]. Available: http://news.bbc.co.uk/1/hi/england/kent/5367478.stm. [Accessed 02 March 2023].

[59] BBC, "Jail building starts unannounced," 30 March 2007. [Online]. Available: http://news.bbc.co.uk/1/hi/england/kent/5367478.stm. [Accessed 02 March 2023].

[60] BBC, "Jail building expansion suspended," 03 April 2007. [Online]. Available: http://news.bbc.co.uk/1/hi/england/kent/6522655.stm. [Accessed 02 March 2023].

[61] Hansard, UK Government, "Volume 461: debated on Wednesday 6 June 2007," 06 June 2007. [Online]. Available: https://hansard.parliament.uk/Commons/2007-06-06/debates/0706073000104/PrisonsRochester. [Accessed 02 March 2023].

[62] BBC, "Jail building decision postponed," 08 August 2007. [Online]. Available:

http://news.bbc.co.uk/1/hi/england/kent/6937903.stm. [Accessed 02 March 2023].

[63] Premier Modular Group, "HMP Rochester," 2008. [Online]. Available: https://premiermodulargroup.co.uk/sectors/mod-moj/hmp-rochester/. [Accessed 02 March 2023].

[64] GOV.UK, "Justice Secretary announces plans to create 5,000 modern prison places," 22 March 2017. [Online]. Available: https://www.gov.uk/government/news/justice-secretary-announces-plans-to-create-5000-modern-prison-places. [Accessed 09 March 2023].

[65] GOV.UK, "Rochester Prison - GOV.UK," 02 August 2022. [Online]. Available: https://www.gov.uk/guidance/rochester-prison. [Accessed 17 April 2023].

[66] IMB, "Annual Report of the Independent Monitoring Board at HMP/YOI Rochester (2022-23)," 2023.

[67] Castles and Fortifications of England and Wales, "Chatham Defences," 2023. [Online]. Available: http://www.ecastles.co.uk/chatham.html. [Accessed 20 February 2023].

[68] Wikipedia, "Royal Commission on the Defence of the United Kingdom," 03 May 2022. [Online]. Available: https://en.wikipedia.org/wiki/Royal_Commission_on_the_Defence_of_the_United_Kingdom. [Accessed 20 February 2023].

[69] R. Lyne, Military Railways in Kent, Maidstone: North Kent Books, 1983.

[70] Royal Engineers Institute, Professional Papers of the Corps of

Royal Engineers, 1883, Vol. 9, 1883.

[71]   T. J. Lodge, "Handyside Locomotives," *The Industrial Railway Record,* vol. 53, pp. 205-219, April 1974.

[72]   Edinburgh Evening News, 18 June 1897.

[73]   Evening Star, p. 3, 22 May 1897.

[74]   The London Standard, 20 January 1897.

[75]   Kent and Sussex Times, 19 October 1878.

[76]   FindaGrave, "Charles Graydon (1857-1878) - FindaGrave," [Online]. Available: https://www.findagrave.com/memorial/224780439/charles-graydon. [Accessed 11 September 2023].

[77]   Durham County Advertiser, p. 3, 01 August 1879.

[78]   K. R. Gulvin, The Medway Forts, Medway, 1976.

[79]   S. G. Small, Fort Bridgewoods, Bedford: Radio Society of Great Britain, 2015.

[80]   Wikipedia, "Norman Gilbert Mitchell-Innes," 15 January 2017. [Online]. Available: https://en.wikipedia.org/wiki/Norman_Gilbert_Mitchell-Innes. [Accessed 20 January 2023].

[81]   Dundee Courier, "Major Blake Fined 250 Guineas," p. 7, 16 December 1926.

[82]   C. Rich, Recollections of a Prison Governor, London: Hurst and Blackwell, 1932.

[83]   The Sun (Auckland), "The Sun," vol. II, no. 424, 4 August 1928.

[84]   N. S. Hayner, "English Schools for Young Offenders," *Journal of Criminal Law and Criminology (1931-1951)*, vol. 27, no. 5, 1937.

[85]   Rochester, Chatham & Gillingham Journal, "Rochester, Chatham & Gillingham Journal," 31 August 1889.

[86]   Rochester, Chatham & Gillingham Journal, "Rochester, Chatham & Gillingham Journal," 18 July 1891.

[87]   Yorkshire Telegraph and Star, p. 3, 01 June 1900.

[88]   Eastern Evening News, 03 December 1900.

[89]   Dundee Evening Post, 30 November 1900.

[90]   London Evening News, p. 3, 05 December 1900.

[91]   St. James's Gazette, p. 8, 07 December 1900.

[92]   The Holloway & Hornsey Press, p. 5, 21 December.

[93]   The Peterborough and Huntingdonshire Standard, p. 3, 26 January 1901.

[94]   Evening Standard, p. 7, 18 April 1901.

[95]   South Eastern Gazette, "South Eastern Gazette," 5 February 1877.

[96]   Western Gazette, "Western Gazette," 27 October 1893.

[97] *The Chatham, Rochester and Gillingham Observer,* pp. 7,10, 10 January 1920.

[98] National Archives, *PCOM 9/564 (Prison Commission),* Kew.

[99] The Battle of Britain Historical Timeline, "Tuesday 8 October 1940," [Online]. Available: https://battleofbritain1940.com/entry/tuesday-8-october-1940/. [Accessed 07 March 2023].

[100] Medway Memories, "At last, the Borstal big gun theory is blown apart," [Online]. Available: https://medwaymemories.co.uk/medway-at-war/at-last-the-borstal-big-gun-theory-is-blown-apart/. [Accessed 07 March 2023].

[101] The Battle of Britain Memorial London, "The Airmen's Stories - Sgt. R A Ward," [Online]. Available: https://www.bbm.org.uk/airmen/WardRA.htm. [Accessed 07 March 2023].

[102] Find a Grave, "Sir Evelyn Ruggles-Brise (1857-1935)," [Online]. Available: https://www.findagrave.com/memorial/248696125/evelyn-john-ruggles-brise. [Accessed 20 January 2023].

Web links that have been used as references may not be accessible after publication of this book. If you find you are unable to access any online resources, please use the Wayback Machine, where old webpages are archived: **https://web.archive.org/**

INDEX

Printed in Great Britain
by Amazon

42083098R00089